BEST OF

Friends

The Unofficial *Friends* Companion

JAE-HA KIM

HarperPerennial

A Division of HarperCollins*Publishers*

This book is dedicated to my mother,
who always believed I was the best,
and to my father, who knew I could do better

HarperCollins books may be purchased for educational, business, or sales promotional use. For information please write: Special Markets Department, HarperCollins Publishers, Inc., 10 East 53rd Street, New York, NY 10022.

FIRST EDITION

DESIGNED BY JOEL AVIROM & JASON SNYDER

ISBN 0-06-095178-8

95 96 97 98 99 ❖/RRD 10 9 8 7 6 5 4

Acknowledgments

★ ★★★ ★

*S*pecial thanks to the following people for their support and their invaluable contributions to this book: Jong-Suk and Sang-Sup Kim, who kept me fed and calm throughout the whole project; Jae-Hu Kim (my brother, the inventor, whose Universal SIMM made my computer printer work *that* much better); my sister Jae-Hi Neill for her enthusiasm; the Neills (Tom, Henna, Christian, Seth, and Elizabeth) and the Kims (Mee Young, Tabitha, and Lisa); and Julie Burros, who can keep a secret better than anyone I know.

Extraspecial thanks to my editor, Mauro DiPreta, who tirelessly juggled work on this book with Lamaze classes—and for whose baby "I will always have gum." Kudos also go out to his ace assistant, Kristen Auclair, who cleverly deciphered all the nonsensical messages I left at two in the morning.

My undying gratitude to my überagent Jane Jordan Browne and her associate Danielle Egan-Miller, both of whom nudged me in the right direction when all I wanted to do was sleep.

And for all *my* friends, who are the real things ...

Introduction

★ ★★★ ★

*F*riends is a phenomenon that doesn't lie in the talent of one star but rather in the chemistry among six actors, none of whom was considered a "name" draw before committing to the series.

But that doesn't mean there aren't favorites. At parties, men always ask me if I've ever met Courteney Cox (Yes, she served me coffee on the set of one of her movies, polite girl that she is), and women always want to know if Matthew Perry is like Chandler (Yes, he might even be funnier off camera).

These days, *all* the Friends are on Hollywood's A-list and are either starring in, or auditioning for, major motion pictures. Perhaps more telling of their fame is that they now have the dubious distinction of sharing tabloid pages with Roseanne, O.J., and Whitney. (Yes, David Schwimmer and Jennifer Aniston are dating—but *not* each other.)

This book is for all the *Friends* fans—both the diehard ones who caught all twenty-four episodes of the debut season and are just itching to find a mistake in this book (I hope not!) and the casual viewers who tune in every now and again to see what the gang is up to.

The 1995–1996 season will include episodes revolving around Ross's new girlfriend, Julie, breastfeeding, Mr. Heckles's death, and Ben's day on a bus. But let's step back a season and recap the year that was.

Have fun!

Prologue

★★★

THE FRIENDS:

Chandler Bing (Matthew Perry)
Phoebe Buffay (Lisa Kudrow)
Monica Geller (Courteney Cox)
Ross Geller (David Schwimmer)
Rachel Green (Jennifer Aniston)
Joey Tribbiani (Matt LeBlanc)

*T*hey sure look like cute couples, don't they?
But Jennifer Aniston, David Schwimmer, Lisa Kudrow,
Matt LeBlanc, Matthew Perry, and Courteney Cox are
just good friends. (Janet Gough/Celebrity Photo Agency)

FRIENDSHIP RING

To understand *Friends,* you have to be familiar with the characters. Each of the following chapters will recap an episode of the 1994–1995 season. But for a quick overview, here's a synopsis of the highlights:

Carol (Jane Sibbett) divorces Ross so that she can live with her lesbian lover, Susan (Jessica Hecht). But Carol is pregnant with Ross's baby. Ross likes Rachel, who left her groom standing at the altar because he reminded her of Mr. Potato Head. Unfortunately, Rachel is hot for Paolo (Cosimo Fusco), an Italian playboy who makes a play for Phoebe. Ross shares a romantic kiss with Mrs. Bing (Morgan Fairchild), who is Chandler's mother. Meanwhile, Chandler ends up on a blind date with his ex-girlfriend Janice (Maggie Wheeler), whom he has already broken up with twice within the past five months. Chandler and Joey share an apartment across the hall from Ross's sister, Monica, and Rachel. At one point or another, most of them have seen each other naked in the shower, though they don't date each other. Joey dates and then gets dumped by Phoebe's twin sister, Ursula (also played by Lisa Kudrow). Carol gives birth to Ross's baby, who has two moms, a dad, and an adoring Aunt Monica who promises the newborn she'll always have gum. When Rachel finally learns that Ross is in love with her, she goes to meet him at the airport. What she doesn't know is that he has returned with another woman.

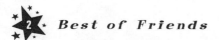

1. "The One Where Monica Gets a Roommate"

★★

Original air date: September 22, 1994

*T*he Friends *gang hangs out at one of two places: their favorite java hut, Central Perk, or Monica's apartment. Make that Monica and Rachel's apartment. After Rachel leaves her Mr. Potato Head–look-alike fiancé at the altar, she moves in with Monica and discovers that independence is a bitch when you don't have Daddy's credit cards to rely on. "Welcome to the real world," Monica says. "It sucks! You're going to love it."*

It sucks, all right. Especially when your best friends are drop-dead good-looking and you're not dating them. Though much has been written about the improbability of six attractive members of the opposite sex *not* dating each other, I can totally understand why these six aren't.

Ross is about to get divorced, so Phoebe and Rachel are wise to stay away from the human guilt magnet. Like they really want to hear him talk about his soon-to-be ex, Carol, while he's on a date with them. I think not. Since Monica's his sister and they're not royalty, dating her is not an option either.

All three of the female Friends could overcome the fact that Joey's dense (for a couple dates, anyhow) because he's got washboard abs and a killer smile, but they probably couldn't get past the fact that he's got H-I-M-B-O written all over his perfect forehead.

And as for Chandler—poor Chandler—he's just too needy. What he *wants* is a partner in life. What he needs is to get a life.

The women fare better on the dateability scale. Monica, Rachel, and Phoebe are all pretty enough to be soap-opera divas. But like many attractive women, they tend to go for men who are nice but not very attractive. In other words—uggos—which rules the *Friends* men out. (Having said that, I will admit that I mentally categorized Ross as an uggo during the first couple of episodes. But his droopy, hangdog looks

3

have grown on me. My friend Julie can't get beyond his nose, which she insists is fake, but that's another story altogether.)

If the male Friends were women, they'd know that Monica was the most desirable of their female Friends. But they're not, so they don't. Not only is Monica beautiful, but she doesn't have a clue about it. She's also smart, neat, and has a great job as a chef. Ruling out her brother, Ross, for obvious reasons, that leaves Chandler and Joey as potential dating partners. Monica had an unrequited crush on Joey that materialized into friendship. As for Chandler, she thought at first that he was gay (not that there's anything wrong with that—oh, sorry—wrong show). Now she pretty much views him as an entertaining eunuch.

Phoebe's too New Agey for these guys. Though she's kind-hearted and a good soul, she's not enough of a babe to make up for the fact that she's a ding-a-ling.

*R*oss wishes he was this chummy with Rachel. In real life, David Schwimmer and Jennifer Aniston are pals and accompanied each other to the premiere of *Before Sunrise.* (Albert Ortega/Celebrity Photo Agency)

Rachel is the one that both Joey and Ross want. Joey's interest in her doesn't go any further than little Joey. Ross, on the other hand, sees a helpless woman whom he can take care of. If Rachel and Ross ever start dating seriously, be prepared for the downfall of the show. Because once they fall in love, the dynamics of *Friends* will be off-kilter. Plus there'll be the inevitable season-finale wedding and then the show will suck and get canceled. Need I say more than *Rhoda?* Don't remember it? My point exactly.

HEAR ME NOW, ROSS: Stay away from Rachel. She's trouble! She's on the rebound! You're too nice for her! *Stay away . . .* for at least another couple of seasons, anyhow.

CLUE PATROL

There's gullible and then there's just plain stupid. During the first episode Monica proves to be both. While on a first date with a colleague, she falls for the old I-haven't-been-able-to-get-it-up-since-my-wife-left-me line and sleeps with him. *Hello?* We've all been there, girlfriend, but most of us haven't fallen for it.

HE SAID/SHE SAID

*"My ideal weight would be a hundred pounds.
My whole family is shaped like pears and I'm afraid
of looking like that."*

**—Courteney Cox, who, at five foot five,
weighs a piggish 108 pounds**

---

*"I can tell you one thing. I certainly won't be as nice
as [Valerie Bertinelli] is when I'm the center of a show.
I'm going to milk it for all it's worth."*

**—Matthew Perry (in 1990), talking about working with nice Bertinelli
on the short-lived series *Sydney***

THE KEATON CONNECTION

Before getting engaged to Michael "Batman" Keaton in real life, Courteney Cox dated Alex Keaton. Okay, Alex wasn't a *real* person but rather the *Family Ties* character played by Michael J. Fox.

*S*orry guys—Courteney Cox is as good as married to longtime boyfriend, Michael Keaton.
(Jim Smeal/Galella Ltd.)

"THE ONE WHERE MONICA GETS A ROOMMATE" QUIZ

1. The gang is watching a Spanish soap opera. When two of the soap actresses start arguing, what do the Friends start chanting?

2. What was the name of the school Rachel and Monica attended together?

3. When Rachel freaks out in Monica's apartment, what song does Phoebe sing to calm her down?

4. What kind of ethnic food do Monica and Paul the Wine Guy eat on their first date?

5. Monica works as a chef at what chic eatery?

6. Which Friend had the most dysfunctional childhood?

7. On what was to have been her honeymoon night, Rachel is home alone. What does she watch on TV?
    a. The *Happy Days* series finale where Joanie and Chachi get hitched
    b. *The Fresh Prince of Bel Air* where the Fresh Prince proposes
    c. The *Petticoat Junction* episode where Betty Joe and Steve get married

8. What cartoon series poster does Ross have on his wall?
   a. *Bugs Bunny*
   b. *Speed Racer*
   c. *Beavis & Butt-Head*

9. Which rock band sings the theme to *Friends*?
   a. The Romantics
   b. The Rembrandts
   c. The Ramones

10. Joey makes a comparison between women and what kind of food?
    a. Cheesecake
    b. Rump roast
    c. Ice cream

"THE ONE WHERE MONICA GETS A ROOMMATE" ANSWERS

1. "Push her down the stairs!"

2. Lincoln High School. Monica's older brother, Ross, also went there.

3. "These Are a Few of My Favorite Things."

4. Japanese

5. Iridium

6. Phoebe. At fourteen, she moved to New York by herself after her mom killed herself and her stepdad was imprisoned. She lived with an albino guy who killed himself. She found her salvation when she discovered aromatherapy.

7. a. The *Happy Days* series finale where Joanie and Chachi get hitched

8. b. *Speed Racer*

9. b. The Rembrandts

10. c. Ice cream

2. "The One with the Sonogram at the End"

★ ★★

Original air date: September 29, 1994

*R*oss's ex-wife, Carol, tells him she is pregnant and wants to give the baby both her and her female lover's last names, but not Ross's. Monica goes on a manic cleaning spree to impress her parents, who favor Ross. Phoebe notes, "You're all chaotic and twirly—and not in a good way." Meanwhile, Rachel finds out that the man she left at the altar went on "their honeymoon" with her maid of honor, Mindy, which makes her feel worse than she does when she sees Ugly Naked Guy in the apartment across the street.

The relationship between Ross and Monica is classic sibling rivalry. No matter how messed up Ross's life is, their mother stirs more poop up and lays it on Monica's teeny shoulders. That Ross is divorced from a lesbian is somehow more comforting to Mrs. Geller than the fact that Monica never married. Their mom can't forgive Monica for being the heavy child she was. Mrs. Geller, basically, is a shrew who probably won't—and shouldn't—be invited to Monica's home unless she learns that manners apply to her, too.

While the nation has proclaimed Ross the sensitive Friend, I must point out that he can be as Neanderthal as the cavemen he writes about in his paleontological papers. When Carol and her lover, Susan, decide to name their baby Helen—if it's a girl—he objects. His baby will *not* be called Helen Geller (get it?), he says, automatically assuming that the child will have his last name. *As if!*

True, it might be traditional. But there's nothing traditional about his relationship with Carol (she's a lesbian, remember?). She's got her own weirdo ideas and wants the baby to take both her and Susan's last names (Willick-Bunch—which sounds like "*well, look, a bunch*"). I don't *think* so. The baby should take Mom's name and just be Baby Willick. (For those of you who don't know the sex and can't stand not knowing, skip ahead to Chapter 12: "The One with the Dozen Lasagnas" to find out whether it's a boy or girl, 'cause I'm not blabbing here.)

I've got to give Rachel her props, though, because she did the mature thing. There are few of us who haven't been cheated on, and though she *did* leave Barry standing at the altar, he rebounded awfully quickly. By returning the engagement ring rather than selling it and buying some more bitchin' Joan & David boots, Rachel is trying to make things right. Even after finding out that Barry consoled himself by treating her maid of honor to a "honeymoon" in Aruba, she gave back the ring.

Where Rachel faltered was by blaming the other woman rather than her ex–Mr. Potato Head man. It would've been more effective if she had told *him*, rather than Mindy, that she hoped their future children would inherit "his old hairline" and Mindy's "old nose." (This last jab is especially relevant since Jennifer Grey, who plays Mindy in a later episode, displays a much smaller, perkier nose than the one she hauled around in *Dirty Dancing*. See Chapter 20: "The One with the Evil Orthodontist" for more.)

THERE'S NO PLACE LIKE HOME

Well, actually, there is. Next time you're in New York, check out 90 Bedford Street (at the corner of Bedford and Grove in New York City). Look familiar? The building's exterior is the one shown on *Friends* and it is where Monica, Rachel, Chandler, and Joey supposedly live. You can't take a tour inside (unless you have *real* friends who live there), but you can stop in for some java and chow at Chez Michallet, the French bistro that's in the building.

And while there's no real Central Perk, David Schwimmer and other *Friends* have been known to hang at Manhattan's trendy World Cafe (201 Columbus Avenue). The wait staff is used to serving celebs—regulars include Eddie Murphy, Joan Lunden, and the man himself, Regis Philbin. But the Friends are by far the most popular. The staff says that not one of them is a troublemaker (yet), and that they're all java junkies, with the exception of tea lover Courteney Cox.

*I*t's not Central Perk, but World Cafe is a must for *Friends* fans. David Schwimmer stopped in regularly for java and jive during his off-time from filming *The Pallbearer*.

TALK THE TALK

> *"I think that for us, kissing is pretty much like an opening act. It's like the stand-up comedian you have to sit through before Pink Floyd comes out."*

—Chandler, on foreplay

THE CHRISTINA PICKLES CONNECTION

Almost a decade before Christina Pickles was cast to play Courteney Cox's mom on *Friends*, the two actresses worked together in the Dolph Lundgren film *Masters of the Universe*. Cox was cast as the teenage ingenue, Julie Winston. Pickles played the Sorceress—only, unlike Mrs. Geller, she was kind all the time. Not that this has anything to do with either one of the actresses, but there was also a character named Monica (played by Jessica Nelson) in the movie.

"THE ONE WITH THE SONOGRAM AT THE END" QUIZ

1. Where does Ross work?

2. What is the name of the actress who plays Carol? (Hint: It's not Jane Sibbett, who currently plays her.)

3. Where does Phoebe find Rachel's engagement ring?
   a. In a pan of lasagna
   b. In the vacuum cleaner
   c. In a bottle of wine

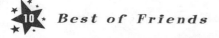

4. What TV show does the gang watch in this episode?

5. If the baby's a girl, Ross wants to name her Julia. Susan likes the name Helen. What are Carol's choices?
   a. Mickey or Maggie
   b. Marlon or Minnie
   c. Mick or Mary

6. Which Friend is an only child?

7. What is Mr. Geller's pet name for Monica?

8. Match the Friend to the reaction he/she has when Ross shows them the sonogram of his baby:

Phoebe	Keeps talking on the phone
Chandler	Cries
Joey	Compares it to an old potato
Monica	Says it looks like something about to attack the *Starship Enterprise*
Rachel	Doesn't know what to look for

*J*ane Sibbett (left) and Jessica Hecht
(lucky girl in between Schwimmer and LeBlanc), who play lovers Carol and Susan,
join the gang at an awards ceremony. (Miranda Shen/Celebrity Photo Agency)

9. What did Ugly Naked Guy purchase?

10. How did Barry improve his looks?

"The One with the Sonogram at the End" Answers

1. Museum of Prehistoric History

2. Anita Barone

3. a. In a pan of lasagna

4. *Three's Company*

5. b. Marlon or Minnie

6. Chandler

7. "Our little harmonica"

8. When Ross shows the Friends the sonogram of his baby:

Phoebe	Compares it to an old potato
Chandler	Says it looks like something about to attack the *Starship Enterprise*
Joey	Doesn't know what to look for
Monica	Cries
Rachel	Keeps talking on the phone

9. A Thigh Master

10. Barry got hair plugs and contact lenses.

3. "The One with the Thumb"

Original air date: October 6, 1994

*C*handler's reunited with his beloved cigarettes, which the rest of the *Friends* can't stand. *Monica dates a man all her buddies love but with whom she's bored. And poor, honest Phoebe can't deal with the fact that her bank gave her one thousand dollars that isn't hers. Plus a soda company gives her seven thousand more unwanted bucks after she finds a dismembered thumb "floating around like a tiny, little hitchhiker" in a can of soda.*

There are three moral dilemmas presented here. Chandler's: To smoke or not to smoke. Monica's: To dump or not to dump. Phoebe's: To keep or not to keep.

Let's start with Monica's. While all her pals are disappointed when she dumps her boyfriend, Alan, I'm quite pleased. Why? Because I hate the fact that gorgeous Monica is dating another dorko guy whose wonderfulness is supposed to make up for the fact that he is just another old, boring, hirsute uggo. (Say what you will about Michael Keaton not deserving Courteney Cox, but at least he's damned funny and looks great in rubber.)

Granted, looks should not be the only barometer for potential mates. But how come only the women date so-so looking guys while the men all go out with gorgeous fantasies? Even Ross—the least classically attractive of the three male Friends—dates only faboo women who look like they've stepped off the covers of fashion magazines. (After his divorce from Carol, Ross—who hasn't been with anyone other than Carol in nine years—dates Kristen [Heather Medway]. Medway had a co-starring role on *Models inc.* as a model wannabe who should've been. For more details, see Chapter 14: "The One with the Candy Hearts.")

Chandler's return to puffing is no surprise. Using the pretense of teaching Joey to smoke for a role, Chandler offers to show him the *right* way to suck on a ciggie. He promises he won't get addicted again. Then he gets addicted. For a second he even invokes the satanic character he played on *Dream On* (the ruthless editor Alex) when he lashes out at Joey and Ross: "I've had it with you guys and your cancer and your emphysema and your heart disease. The bottom line is, smoking is cool and you know it."

Now the Phoebe factor is another story altogether. While honesty is the best policy, I can think of only a handful of people (starting with Mother Teresa and ending with my sister) who would actually give that much money back to a bank. Give back a total of $8,000? *Pish!*

Giving some of the money to a homeless woman was a good deed. Promising the "thumb" money to Chandler was sheer idiocy. *She* found the digit in the can. Finders keepers . . .

TALK THE TALK

> *"They're like coyotes picking off the weak members of the herd."*

—Monica, on how harshly the Friends judge her dates

*U*nlike Chandler who gives up puffing, Matthew Perry has yet to kick the habit even though he looks pretty cool *without* a filter tip, little buddy.
(Bob Sebree/Outline)

Superman Says

"The One with the Thumb" Quiz

1. When Ross and Monica's childhood dog died, how did their parents break the bad news to them?
a. They told the kids that the dog went to live at the Millners' farm in Connecticut.
b. They told them their dog was in heaven with great-grandmama.
c. They told them that the doggie ran away because they were bad kids.

2. Chandler helps Joey rehearse for a prison drama by playing what role?
a. A warden
b. An inmate
c. A priest

3. How long was Chandler smoke-free before he took up the habit again?

4. When Phoebe tells her bank they credited too much money to her account, what does the bank do?
a. Open another account for her
b. Apologize and give her more money, plus a football phone
c. Threaten to sue her for cheating the bank

5. How does Phoebe purge herself of the unwanted money?

6. Match the Friend with his/her idiosyncrasy:

Joey	emits snorts during laughing fits
Ross	gets orders mixed up
Monica	instigates arguments
Phoebe	knuckle cracker
Rachel	overpronounces words
Chandler	hair chewer

*L*isa Kudrow shows off her new hairstyle at the *2nd Annual VH-1 Honors* ceremony that she cohosted with Jennifer Aniston in June 1995.
(Jim Smeal/Galella Ltd.)

7. Chandler loves Alan's David Hasselhoff imitations.
True   False

8. What is Lizzy the Homeless Woman's nickname for Phoebe?
a. Space Cadet
b. Bat Girl
c. Weird Girl

9. What does Alan say when Monica tells him it's over?
a. "Is it all right if I ask Rachel out?"
b. "I can't stand your friends."
c. "You're a bitch."

10. How do the Friends console themselves after Monica dumps Alan?

1. a. They told the kids that the dog went to live at the Millners' farm in Connecticut.

2. a. A warden

3. Three years

4. b. Apologize and give her more money, plus a football phone

5. Phoebe gives Lizzy the Homeless Woman the $1,000 that the bank mistakenly gave her. And she makes a deal with Chandler: If he'll stop smoking, she'll give him the $7,000 the soda company gave her.

6. The Friends' idiosyncrasies are:

Joey	knuckle cracker
Ross	over pronounces words
Monica	emits snorts during laughing fits
Phoebe	hair chewer
Rachel	gets orders mixed up
Chandler	instigates arguments

7. True

8. c. Weird Girl

9. b. "I can't stand your friends."

10. They pig-out on Häagen-Dazs ice cream and cheesecake.

4. "The One with George Stephanopoulos"

★ ★

Original air date: October 13, 1994

*W*hen Pizza Guy accidentally delivers a pizza meant for George Stephanopoulos—who lives across the street—to the female Friends, the women decide to peek at the towel-clad former White House adviser with their binoculars (much better than Ugly Naked Guy). Meanwhile, Chandler and Joey take Ross, who is mourning the night he lost his virginity to Carol, to a hockey game.

One of the reasons why women like Ross so much is the exact same reason why Chandler makes fun of him: He has slept with only one woman—Carol—and he was in love with her.

Ross is the only Friend who equates sex with love, and it's a sweet quality. Do guys like that actually exist? Sure they do. Do I know any of them? No, I don't.

Ross is a throwback to the days when men courted women. When he offers to do nice things for women (like sweeping the floor or sorting their laundry), he doesn't consider it foreplay. While *Friends* hasn't delved into the dynamics of Ross and Carol's divorce, it's clear that the dissolution of their marriage had more to do with her coming to terms with her lesbianism than his being a poor husband.

Ross is a paleontologist. He works in a museum, writes scientific papers, and goes to China to examine ancient artifacts. It's safe to assume that he went to a good university. If any of the other Friends went to college, it was probably to escape reality. Chandler works in data processing, but as a permanent temp, which makes me wonder about his drive. And I think it's a good bet that if Joey went to college at all, it was probably to Volleyball U.

Ross is the only intellectual in a group of slackers, which may be one reason why he doesn't tout how smart he is. He wants to fit in.

Monica was an outcast in high school because she was a big, fat tubbo. I get the feeling that Ross probably was a high school nebbish, too, and was more popular with the projectionist/chess crowd than the football/cheerleader squad.

And while smart women want smart men who are their equals, smart men don't mind dim, pretty bracelets, which is why Ross is so hot for a woman like Rachel, who thinks George Stephanopoulos is a babe but has no idea who he is.

*D*avid Schwimmer is an award-winning theater director who cofounded Chicago's Lookingglass Theatre Company.
(John Paschal/Celebrity Photo Agency)

MONEY, THAT'S WHAT I WANT

As with all of us and our friends, some of the Friends have jobs while the others have careers. Take a look:

Ross: Paleontologist
Monica: Chef
Chandler: Data processor
Rachel: Waitress
Joey: Actor-model
Phoebe: Masseuse

"The One with George Stephanopoulos"

FRIENDS TAPINGS

If you're in California or plan to be in California and want to see a taping of *Friends,* send a self-addressed, stamped envelope to: Audiences Unlimited, 100 Universal City Plaza, Building 153, Universal City, CA, 91605. (Be sure to specify that you want to see *Friends* or they might send you to *The Tonight Show* instead. Tix are also available at the Fox Television Center, 5746 Sunset Boulevard (a block west of the 101 Hollywood freeway). Tix are free but may be difficult to get due to the popularity of the show. Still, it can't hurt to try. For more info call (818) 506-0067.

"THE ONE WITH GEORGE STEPHANOPOULOS" QUIZ

1. How many steps is it from Joey and Chandler's apartment to Central Perk?

2. When Chandler and Joey take Ross to the hockey game, which team are the New York Rangers playing?

3. Pizza Guy mixed up the Friends' and Stephanopoulos's orders. The girls ended up with his mushroom, green pepper, and onion pizza. What kind had they ordered?
a. Low-fat cheese and spinach
b. Pepperoni and olives
c. Fat-free crust with extra cheese

4. What do Joey and Chandler promise to buy Ross at the hockey game?

5. By how much time are Joey and Chandler off in taking Ross out to celebrate his birthday?
a. Seven days
b. Seven weeks
c. Seven months

6. What day and month did Ross and Carol first do it?

7. Match the Friend to the right answer: "If I were omnipotent for a day, I would want . . . "

Phoebe	". . . world peace, no more hunger, good things for the rain forest."
Chandler	". . . I'd probably kill myself."
Joey	". . . I'd make myself omnipotent forever."

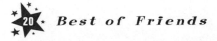

A baby-faced Matthew Perry on the set of *Sydney* in 1990.

(Jim Smeal/Galella Ltd.)

8. After Ross stops a hockey puck with his face, what does Chandler do when he notices they're on TV?
   a. Screams out for an ambulance
   b. Mouths, "Hi, Mom"
   c. Shouts, "Hey, we're on that TV thing!"

9. What does Phoebe say when she sees Stephanopoulos's date eat a slice of pizza?
   a. "Hey, that's not for you, bitch."
   b. "She's got cheese hanging out of her mouth."
   c. "Eww—she dripped sauce all over his futon."

10. Phoebe brought Operation over but the gang can't play the game because the tweezers are missing. So what do they play instead?
    a. Twister
    b. Monopoly
    c. Clue

"THE ONE WITH GEORGE STEPHANOPOULOS" ANSWERS

1. 97

2. Pittsburgh Penguins

3. c. Fat-free crust with extra cheese

4. A Big Thumb Finger

5. c. Seven months

6. October 20

7. "If I were omnipotent for a day, I would want . . . "

Phoebe	". . . world peace, no more hunger, good things for the rain forest." (She also said "and bigger boobs" but I thought that would give it away.)
Chandler	". . . I'd make myself omnipotent forever."
Joey	". . . I'd probably kill myself." (He gets omnipotent and impotent mixed up.)

8. c. Shouts, "Hey, we're on that TV thing!"

9. a. "Hey, that's not for you, bitch."

10. a. Twister

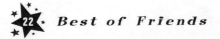

5. "The One with the East German Laundry Detergent"

****

Original air date: October 20, 1994

Joey wants to get back together with a former girlfriend he dumped, so he makes Monica pose as his new gal pal. Ross helps Rachel, a laundry virgin, do her first load of wash. And Chandler has a difficult time breaking up with Janice. Joey's advice: "Why do you have to break up with her? Be a man. Just stop calling her."

As Rachel points out, guys can pee standing up but are incapable of doing so many other things—like calling. Joey's method of dumping by silence may be the coward's way out, but it's also a very effective one.

When a guy stops calling, it may hurt in the beginning but you get over it. Ultimately, you and your friends have a field day reveling in his lameness. Personally, I think you get over this kind of breakup a lot quicker than when he tries to be nice about it and gives you the lame-o "let's be friends" speech. Let's not, and pretend you're dead instead.

The reason Chandler will be bumping heads with Janice in the future is because he is so unfinal about their breakup. He says he wants to break up with her, but then he hems and haws about it for hours before and after he actually gets the words out. And to Janice that means he's not sure.

She'll be back. And I can't wait.

A LITTLE TOO SOON

Hawk-eyed *Friends* viewers will notice a sequencing problem with this episode. While on a double date Monica tells a funny story about an Underdog balloon that got away. That balloon was actually part of a

Thanksgiving parade and played an important role in ruining Monica's holiday dinner. *That* episode won't be shown for four more weeks (see Chapter 9: "The One Where Underdog Gets Away"). So unless Monica is clairvoyant, there is no way she could've known at this time that Underdog was going to make a run for it.

"THE ONE WITH THE EAST GERMAN LAUNDRY DETERGENT" QUIZ

1. What kind of fabric softener does Ross use?

2. What laundry detergent does Ross share with Rachel?

3. Not knowing that Chandler's about to dump her, what does Janice give Chandler?
   a. A Coach briefcase
   b. A pair of Bullwinkle socks
   c. A bag of chocolate Kisses

4. What does Rachel's father offer her if she'll move back home?
   a. A Mercedes convertible
   b. A shopping spree at Neiman Marcus
   c. A month-long trip to Paris

5. Ugly Naked Guy is laying kitchen tile.
   True   False

6. Rachel's first batch of laundry is a success.
   True   False

7. What is the name of the woman Joey wants to date again?
   a. Antoinette
   b. Fifi
   c. Angela

8. When Joey tells an ex-girlfriend she looks good, what does she say?
   a. "That's because I'm wearing a dress that accents my boobs."
   b. Nothing
   c. "Thank you, Joeykins."

9. Phoebe makes a pact with Chandler to break up with her boyfriend, Tony, on the same night he breaks up with Janice.
   True   False

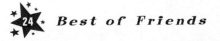

10. At which restaurant do Joey and Monica meet Bob and Angela?
   a. Riff's
   b. Iridium
   c. Fiorello's

"THE ONE WITH THE EAST GERMAN LAUNDRY DETERGENT" ANSWERS

1. Snuggles

2. Überweiss

3. b. A pair of Bullwinkle socks

4. a. A Mercedes convertible

5. True

6. False. She washes a red sock with her whites that turns her load of laundry pink.

7. c. Angela

8. a. "That's because I'm wearing a dress that accents my boobs."

9. True

10. c. Fiorello's

*M*att LeBlanc and Matthew Perry—two of the three best-looking guys on *Friends.*
(John Paschal/Celebrity Photo Agency)

6. "The One with the Butt"

★★

Original air date: October 27, 1994

*J*oey gets his big film break when he's hired to be Al Pacino's stunt butt. When he loses the gig, Phoebe cheers him up by promising that one day a fledgling actor will say, "I got the part! I got the part! I'm going to be Joey Tribbiani's ass." Chandler has second thoughts about an exotic, married woman who wants him to be her sex toy. Meanwhile, Monica tries hard to prove to her friends that she really doesn't have a type-A personality and can be as kooky as the next anal-retentive chef.

Forget Joey's butt for a second. The real issue here is Rachel's new bitchin' hairstyle that *no one* has commented on.

It's one thing for the producers to slip in another actress to play Carol without making any mention of a facelift or something. But when a major babe like Rachel cuts her locks into a trendsetting do, you'd think the writers would add a few lines from her Friends to comment on it.

In real life there is no way a woman could get her hair totally revamped and not hear at least a peep from someone. Wait, let me rephrase that. Guys like Joey and Chandler may not notice, but lovelorn Ross surely would, as would Phoebe and Monica.

Having said all that, did anyone else notice that Joey obviously *wasn't* naked in the shower scenes when he still had the gig as Pacino's butt double? I know this is TV and they can't get away with showing us Joey's real tush (unless, of course, he lands a gig on *NYPD Blue*), but in the silhouette you can see that he has on a pair of loose-fitting trunks. At least they could've put him in a Speedo so that we could pretend we're seeing something we really want to see, even if we aren't.

STAY WITH ME

Monica is the one who has lived with the most Friends. As children, she and Ross lived in the same house. Monica and Phoebe were college roommates, and now she's living with Rachel, her high school buddy. As for the other Friends, Phoebe lives with her grandmother and her nana's grand man *du soir*, Chandler rooms with Joey, and Ross bunks with Marcel the Monkey (for a while, anyway).

*L*ike her TV character, Courteney Cox admits she's a neat freak.
(Carlo Dalla Chiesa/Outline)

I KNOW YOU

Matthew Perry didn't star in *Cafe Americain*, but his *Sydney* co-star Valerie Bertinelli did. And so did Sofia Milos, who plays Chandler's perfect woman in this episode.

JUST LIKE MOM

Monica's Achilles heel is her mother. And her Friends know it. So when they want to hurt her, they compare her to Mrs. Geller. In this episode Ross accuses Monica of turning into their mother. In "The One

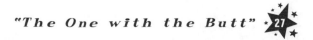

with Two Parts (Part II)," Rachel accuses Monica of being just like Mrs. Geller. And in "The One with the Ick Factor," Monica admonishes herself for sounding like her mother. And yet Monica is so anxious to *be* a mother. What gives?

TALK THE TALK

> *"When I'm with a woman, I need to know that I'm going out with more people than she is."*

—Joey

"THE ONE WITH THE BUTT" QUIZ

1. What color is Monica's bedroom phone?
   a. Red
   b. White
   c. Black

2. In order to prep for his role as Al Pacino's butt double, what does Joey borrow from Monica?
   a. Moisturizer
   b. Makeup
   c. Self-tanning lotion

3. What is the name of Chandler's love interest?

4. What are the names of her husband and two lovers?
   a. Rick, Ethan, and Andrew
   b. Joey, Mark, and Dolph
   c. Sam, Paolo, and Steve

5. Joey stars in which play?
   a. *Jung!*
   b. *Nietsche!*
   c. *Freud!*

6. When Joey tries to add more "personality" by clenching his butt for a shower scene, what does the director say?
   a. "That's amazing, Sparky!"
   b. "Hey, Butt Guy. What the hell are you doing?"
   c. "What else can you wiggle?"

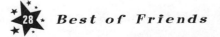

7. After seeing Joey in one of his awful plays for the first time, what does Rachel say to herself?
a. "I feel violated."
b. "He's really talented."
c. "He is so not good."

8. What is the name of Joey's talent agency?

9. How many years has Joey been doing theater?

10. Chandler has a basketball hoop hamper in his bedroom.
True   False

"THE ONE WITH THE BUTT" ANSWERS

1. b. White

2. a. Moisturizer

3. Aurora

4. a. Rick, Ethan, and Andrew

5. c. *Freud!*

6. b. "Hey, Butt Guy. What the hell are you doing?"

7. a. "I feel violated."

8. Estelle Leonard Talent Agency

9. Six years

10. True

7. "The One with the Blackout"

★★★

Original air date: November 3, 1994

*J*ust as Phoebe's about to sing miserable folk songs at Central Perk, New York has a blackout. The gang returns to Monica and Rachel's apartment, where Ross is about to tell Rachel he likes her. "She has no idea what you're thinking," an astute Joey tells him. Meanwhile, Chandler is stuck in an ATM vestibule with Victoria's Secret model Jill Goodacre, whom he tries to impress with lines like "Gum would be perfection."

*A*nd don't they look nice. Matthew Perry, Jennifer Aniston,
and David Schwimmer are decked out for the People's Choice Awards.
(Miranda Shen/Celebrity Photo Agency)

Rachel is so not interested in Ross. Even Joey knows this. When Ross mistakes her platonic affection for burgeoning romance, Joey bursts his bubble with, "It's never going to happen . . . because you waited too long to make your move and now you're in the friend zone."

He's right. Had Ross made his move during the second episode (you'll recall that he laid down the dating groundwork during the season premiere when he asked Rachel if it'd be all right if he asked her out sometime, and she said yes), the two might be a couple—or at least a broken-up couple by this point. But by now Rachel thinks of him as a big brother, not a lover.

And why should she? He never officially asked her out. He doesn't flirt with her (drooling doesn't count). And, for Pete's sake, he never even complimented her on her new hairdo! She'd have to be pretty full of herself to assume he likes her.

Rachel may be a lot of things, but overly confident isn't one of them. Her breakup with Barry left her a little shaky. And though no mention is made of how long the two were a pair before she hauled ass from the altar, I get the impression that they've known each other since childhood—perhaps high school sweethearts.

So when she meets a stunning Italian neighbor during the blackout, it's easy to understand why she falls so hard for him. First, she's still on the rebound. Second, he's got a butt you could bounce quarters off of. And third, he's got a foreign accent, which is always a nice touch. (He's also got a cat, which I could've told you is a bad omen for any potential boyfriend. See Chapter 12: "The One with the Dozen Lasagnas.")

No wonder Ross gets jealous and calls Paolo a "crap weasel."

THE VICTORIA'S SECRET CONNECTION

The *Friends* team recruited two Victoria's Secret models for its debut season. Besides Jill Connick (née Jill Goodacre), who appears as Chandler's dream girl in this episode, Lara Harris has a guest-starring role as the Obsession Girl (see Chapter 9: "The One Where Underdog Gets Away") who thinks Joey has VD. Harris fans will recall that the model guest starred as herself on Fox's canceled *Models inc.*

ITALIAN STALLIONS

Paolo isn't the only Italian stud on the show. So are Matt LeBlanc (even though his last name, which translates into "white," is French) and his alter ego, Joey. Both Matt's and Joey's moms were born in Italy.

*M*att LeBlanc shows off the look that made him a great model.
(Albert Ortega/Galella Ltd.)

"THE ONE WITH THE BLACKOUT" QUIZ

1. Chandler is unable to get money from the ATM because of the blackout.
True   False

2. What is Chandler's bank account number?
a. 7143457
b. 6666666
c. 2435761

3. Match the Friend with the weirdest place he/she had sex:

Monica	Foot of the bed
Joey	Milwaukee
Phoebe	Women's room on the second floor of the New York City Public Library
Ross	Senior year of college on a pool table
Rachel	Disneyland's "It's a Small World" ride

4. What does Phoebe say about Paolo?
a. "I just want to bite his bottom lip. . . . But I won't."
b. "What language does he speak?"
c. "He lives here?!"

5. What is the name of Chandler's bank?

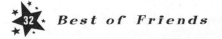

6. Which '70s song are Joey, Monica, and Phoebe singing during the blackout?
a. "Billy, Don't Be a Hero"
b. "American Pie"
c. "On Top of the World"

7. Phoebe and Rachel try to return a lost cat. Whose cat does it turn out to be?
a. The Melons'
b. Mr. Heckles's, who says the cat's name is Bob Buttons
c. Paolo's

8. Phoebe's pet name for the cat is Tootie.
True   False

9. How does Jill Goodacre save Chandler's life?

10. Phoebe blurts out a secret that Monica didn't want Joey to know. What is it?
a. That Monica was a virgin until she was twenty-four
b. That Monica had a crush on Joey when he moved in
c. That Monica made out with Chandler once

"THE ONE WITH THE BLACKOUT" ANSWERS

1. False. He gets money from the machine right before the blackout.

2. a. 7143457

3. Weirdest place they had sex:

Monica	Senior year of college on a pool table
Joey	Women's room on second floor of New York City Public Library
Phoebe	Milwaukee
Ross	Disneyland's "It's a Small World" ride
Rachel	Foot of the bed

4. a. "I just want to bite his bottom lip. . . . But I won't."

5. Emerson Bank

6. c. "On Top of the World"

7. c. Paolo's

8. True

9. She gives him the Heimlich maneuver

10. b. That Monica had a crush on Joey when he moved in

"The One with the Blackout" 33

8. "The One Where Nana Dies Twice"

****

Original air date: November 10, 1994

*M*onica and Ross mourn the death of their grandmother Nana, and Monica and Mrs. Geller come to an unspoken understanding about the relationship between mothers and daughters. Meanwhile, Chandler's irritated by office speculation that he's gay. As Monica tells him, "You have a quality."

Who doesn't have at least one male friend that all your other friends are just *positive* is gay, even if he only dates women? That's the predicament Chandler is in, though I never would have pegged him as preferring men. He likes women too much, which his homosexual colleague, Lowell, picks up right away on his gaydar.

Sure, Chandler shares all the stereotypical qualities that gay men supposedly have. He's neat, slim, smart, and bitchy— but he's also a would-be womanizer at heart. Though Chandler isn't confident about his prowess in the bedroom, he lusts after women in a major way. As Rachel notes, Chandler's the type of guy who'll talk to your breasts all night. (This is perfectly depicted in "The One Where the

*C*ourteney Cox at a Hollywood party in 1988.
(Shell/Galella Ltd.)

Monkey Gets Away," when he and Joey run into a couple of beautiful, sweaty neighbors whom he bludgeons with his verbal horniness.)

And yet even though he's offended that people think he's gay, Chandler doesn't like the idea that he'd be set up with normal-looking Lowell when another colleague (Brian) is so much more attractive.

As for Monica and her mom, they're experiencing a minor break-through in their relationship. In "The One with the Butt," Ross told Monica that she was turning into their mother. In this episode it's obvious that Mrs. Geller treats Monica the same way Nana treated her. Though she's still not a likable character, Mrs. Geller is becoming human and less of a gross cari-cature for viewers to hate.

That role is being saved for the damned monkey, Marcel. (See Chapter 10: "The One with the Monkey.")

A LITTLE TOO SOON

Sequence alert! When Chandler tells the Friends that someone at work thought he was gay, Rachel admits that she thought so, too, when they first met. But she says that when he spent the entire night talking to her breasts at Phoebe's birthday party, she knew he was straight. But Rachel never met Chandler or any of Monica and Ross's friends until *after* she became roommates with Monica. So she couldn't have fêted at any of Phoebe's previous birthdays. And Phoebe won't be celebrating her next b-day till much later (see Chapter 17: "The One with Two Parts (Part II"), which means that there definitely was a booboo in this episode.

AND YOU WOULD BE . . .

When they shot this funeral episode, David Schwimmer had no idea that he would be starring in *The Pallbearer*, his first post-*Friends* film. He plays a man who is asked to be a pallbearer for a guy he doesn't remember. The plot isn't new—it's been used in various incarnations, including on an episode of *Wings* when a high school classmate that Joe Hackett (Tim Daly) doesn't remember asks him to be his best man.

In any case, the theater-trained actor is the busiest of all the Friends. Besides being the first Friend to be recruited for a commercial (AT&T), Schwimmer was courted by no less than four major production companies during the summer of 1995. Each offered a minimum of $1 million per picture. Not too shabby for a guy who once co-starred in the Henry Winkler clunker of a sitcom, *Monty*.

"THE ONE WHERE NANA DIES TWICE" QUIZ

1. Match the Friend to the incident at Nana's funeral:

Monica	Brings a TV to the funeral
Phoebe	Talks about a cute guy, not knowing the guy has just walked into the room
Rachel	Accidentally triggers Ross's muscle spasm
Joey	Falls into a grave ditch
Ross	Steps in mud while wearing new Italian shoes
Chandler	Has hairstyle war with Mrs. Geller

2. Which of Ross and Monica's other relatives are dead?
a. Pop Pop and Aunt Phyllis
b. Aunt Iris
c. Papa and Aunt Mimi

3. What was the name of the coffeehouse Nana and her friends used to hang out at when they were the Friends' age?
a. Central Perk
b. Java Joe's
c. Central Java

4. While in Italy, what does Paolo send Rachel?
a. A romantic love letter
b. A pair of Italian shoes
c. A plane ticket to meet him in Florence

5. Yellow pencils remind Phoebe of her dead friend Debbie.
True   False

6. How many painkillers does Ross take at Nana's funeral?

7. What did Nana used to pilfer wherever she went?

8. At the funeral Chandler meets a beautiful woman named Andrea with whom he starts a short-lived romance.
True   False

9. Ross tells Rachel he loves her.
True   False

10. What was Chandler eating in the office lunchroom?

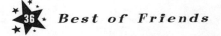

Best of Friends

"THE ONE WHERE NANA DIES TWICE" ANSWERS

1. At Nana's funeral:

Monica	Has hairstyle war with Mrs. Geller
Phoebe	Accidentally triggers Ross's muscle spasm
Rachel	Steps in mud while wearing new Italian shoes
Joey	Brings a TV to the funeral
Ross	Falls into a grave ditch
Chandler	Talks about a cute guy, not knowing the guy has just walked into the room

2. a. Pop Pop and Aunt Phyllis

3. b. Java Joe's

4. b. A pair of Italian shoes

5. True

6. Four

7. Sweet'n Low

8. False. He meets Andrea, who is definitely interested, but whose friend thinks he's gay.

9. True. Still loopy from the painkillers, Ross tells Rachel how he really feels: "I love you the most." But she thinks it's the medication talking and humors him.

10. Instant ramen noodles

9. "The One Where Underdog Gets Away"

★★★

Original air date: November 17, 1994

*M*onica's first Thanksgiving dinner for the Friends burns when they all run to the rooftop to see the runaway Underdog balloon. Joey wins his first modeling gig as the poster boy for VD. Meanwhile, Ross competes with Susan to "communicate" with his unborn baby.

If this episode rings of déjà vu, it's because it's been done before on just about every sitcom imaginable. The most memorable, though, was on an episode of *That Girl,* when Ann Marie cooked a turkey and a goose to appease both her parents and Donald's folks. Because her oven was too small to bake both birds, she ran back and forth between her kitchen and a neighbor's and ended up with the same burned meal Monica couldn't serve up.

But the familiar plot doesn't stop "The One Where Underdog Gets Away" from being one of the season's best. Anyone who has a roommate or ever had a roommate can attest to the fact that signals get mixed all the time. In this episode Monica's beautiful Thanksgiving dinner burns because she and Rachel misunderstand each other. Did Monica actually ask Rachel, "Got the keys?" as they ran out the door, or did she tell her, "Got the keys."? It's a tough call. But since Monica has a better track record than Rachel for being reliable, I've got to place the blame on Rachel.

The little moral is that good friends are better than a great meal. At the end, the happy, satisfied Friends toast one another with, "Here's to a lousy Christmas . . . and a crappy New Year."

Be careful what you wish for, guys, 'cause it just might come true. (See Chapter 10: "The One with the Monkey.")

*M*att LeBlanc—
Could he *be* any cuter?
(Stephen Danelian/Outline)

ROLE MODELS

Joey makes his modeling debut in this episode. In real life, both Matt LeBlanc and Courteney Cox were models before launching their acting careers. Prior to *Friends,* LeBlanc was best known for his Levi's 501 jeans ads and Milky Way commercials, which he took over from Sasha Mitchell, another former model, who went on to co-star in the ABC series *Step By Step.* Before putting his face to work, LeBlanc used his hands as a carpenter to pay his rent. And, unlike Joey, LeBlanc never modeled for any VD posters.

Cox quit Mount Vernon College in Washington, D.C., to model. At five foot five she was too short to do high fashion, but just right to pose for the covers of teen romance novels. She also starred in a series of Noxzema commercials that helped pay for acting lessons. But her breakthrough "role" was a twenty-one-second spot in Bruce Springsteen's "Dancing in the Dark" video. She played an adorable adoring fan who got to dance onstage with the Boss.

Oh, Matthew Perry was never a human hanger, but he comes from model genes. His dad, John Bennett Perry, was the Old Spice guy in TV commercials.

1. Match the Friend to the food he/she requests at Thanksgiving dinner:

      Joey   mashed potatoes with lumps

   Chandler   Tater Tots

      Ross   grilled cheese sandwiches

    Phoebe   mashed potatoes with peas and onions

2. What is the name of Joey's VD poster boy?

a. Mario

b. Joey

c. Serge

3. Embarrassed by being known as the VD poster boy, Joey rips off the bottom of a subway poster, which was plastered over several other promo posters. Which logo was not at the bottom of any of the posters?

a. BLADDER CONTROL PROBLEM

b. STOP WIFE BEATING

c. HEMORRHOIDS

d. WINNER OF THREE TONY AWARDS

e. STOP BEDWETTING

4. What TV show's theme song is Ross singing to Carol's stomach when their baby makes its first kick?

a. *The Brady Bunch*

b. *The Monkees*

c. *The Partridge Family*

5. Why are Monica and Ross having Thanksgiving without their parents?

a. Mr. and Mrs. Geller are going to Puerto Rico for the holiday.

b. Mr. Geller had a heart attack and Mrs. Geller is staying at the hospital with him.

c. Mrs. Geller vows never to spend a holiday with her children until one of them (i.e., Monica) gets married.

6. Why is Thanksgiving such a horrific holiday for Chandler?

7. After breaking away near Macy's, the Underdog balloon flies over Washington Square Park.

   True   False

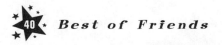

8. How many kinds of potatoes is Monica making for Thanksgiving dinner?
a. One
b. Two
c. Three

9. What is Ugly Naked Guy doing for Thanksgiving?

10. Mr. Heckles joins the Friends for Thanksgiving dinner.
True   False

"THE ONE WHERE UNDERDOG GETS AWAY" ANSWERS

1. The Friends' Thanksgiving dinner requests:

Joey	Tater Tots
Chandler	grilled cheese sandwiches
Ross	mashed potatoes with lumps
Phoebe	mashed potatoes with peas and onions

2. a. Mario

3. e. STOP BEDWETTING

4. b. *The Monkees*

5. a. Mr. and Mrs. Geller are going to Puerto Rico for the holiday.

6. Because that's when his parents told him they were getting divorced—right after he finished his pumpkin pie.

7. True

8. c. Three

9. Spending it with Ugly Naked Gal

10. False. Mr. Heckles doesn't appear in this episode.

10. "The One with the Monkey"

****

Original air date: December 15, 1994

*T*he gang makes and breaks a pact to celebrate New Year's Eve without dates. As Chandler says, they are "sick of being a victim of this Dick Clark holiday." Ross compensates for his loneliness by getting a roommate—a monkey named Marcel whom everyone adores. Well, everyone except Monica, who can't get past the feces-throwing thing. Meanwhile, Phoebe faces a difficult decision when she meets a shy physicist who's thinking about giving up a fellowship in Minsk to stay with her.

*T*he gang that works together wins awards together.
(Janet Gough/Celebrity Photo Agency)

In this episode, we see that Phoebe may be the only Friend who would sacrifice her happiness for someone she loves. When David, her Scientist Guy, offers to give up a three-year grant to work on scientific stuff with his colleague, Max, in Russia to stay with her, she encourages him to go even though she really wants him to stay. Phoebe knows that's what he really wants. But she also knows that if he doesn't snatch this opportunity, there'll always be a part of him that'll blame her for holding him back, which is why she tells him, "You are so going to Minsk."

It's been said that who you ring in the new year with is the person with whom you'll spend the rest of the year. Even though the Friends brought dates to Monica and Rachel's NYE bash, they're all basically alone when the clock strikes twelve. But what they don't seem to realize is that they're alone together.

TALK THE TALK

> *"Hey, that monkey's got a Ross on its ass."*

—Chandler, after seeing Marcel sitting on Ross's shoulder

MONKEY BUSINESS

There's a little bit of cross-dressing going on with the Friends, and no, it has nothing to do with Chandler (even though he does have a certain *quality*). Marcel is played by a female monkey named, coincidentally enough, Monkey, and her lesser-paid double, Katy. For a *Victor/Victoria* take on Marcel, check out Chapter 19: "The One Where the Monkey Gets Away," quiz question number 8.

While the critter looked cute on-screen, Monkey was easily the most despised actress on the set. Sure, all stars throw occasional temper tantrums, but few throw their own feces around. In any case, Marcel's role got written out. Why? It's a combination of two things: the role had pretty much run its course, *plus* Monkey became the first Friend to parlay her sitcom success into a role in a hit feature film (*Outbreak*).

Feces throwing notwithstanding, Matt LeBlanc obviously holds no prejudice against simians. In his first post-*Friends* film *Ed*, which he shot in Canyon Country, California, LeBlanc plays a minor league pitcher whose third baseman is a chimpanzee. Of course this chimp is animatronic.

"The One with the Monkey"

On a related note, Vincent Ventresca (who guest-starred as Monica's New Year's Eve date, Fun Bobby, in "The One with the Monkey") was featured as an anthropologist who tried to decipher a gorilla's soda request in a Pepsi commercial.

"THE ONE WITH THE MONKEY" QUIZ

1. Phoebe's thirteen-song set at Central Perk includes twelve numbers about her mother's suicide and one about . . .
   a. . . . a snowman
   b. . . . a cute guy
   c. . . . Ugly Naked Guy

2. When Chandler baby-sits Marcel, what does the monkey do?
   a. Throws up on him
   b. Amuses him by juggling balled-up socks
   c. Cries until Ross comes home

3. Ross got Marcel after his friend Bethel rescued the monkey from a lab.
   True   False

4. What are David and Max arguing about during Phoebe's acoustic set at Central Perk?
   a. Whether Einstein was more brilliant than Kirkegaard
   b. Whether Daryl Hannah is more attractive than Phoebe
   c. Whether Rachel is worse than the waitress who spilled chili on them at dinner

5. Why is Fun Bobby crying?
   a. He liked Monica better when she was fat.
   b. His grandfather died two hours ago.
   c. He couldn't get his hair to lie just so.

6. What does Max call Phoebe?

7. Who's the first to break the dateless New Year's Eve pact? (Hint: Ross doesn't count since his "date" was simian and not human.)

8. What does Marcel do to Monica's coffee table?
   a. He urinates on it.
   b. He defecates on it.
   c. He plays with himself on it.

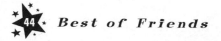

9. Joey is once again playing Santa Claus at the department store this holiday.

True   False

10. When are David and Max supposed to leave for Minsk, if they decide to take the offer?

"THE ONE WITH THE MONKEY" ANSWERS

1. a. . . . a snowman

2. b. Amuses him by juggling balled-up socks

3. True

4. b. Whether Daryl Hannah is more attractive than Phoebe

5. b. His grandfather died two hours ago.

6. Yoko

7. Phoebe is first, then Chandler, Monica, Joey, and Rachel.

8. a. He urinates on it.

9. False. Joey is demoted to one of Santa's elves this year.

10. January 1, 1995

 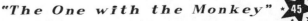

11. "The One with Mrs. Bing"

****

Original air date: January 5, 1995

*C*handler's romance novelist mom comes to New York to visit him and he's not sure how he feels about it, especially after she sucks face with his best friend, Ross, the "mother kisser." Meanwhile, Monica and Phoebe compete for the "attention" of Coma Guy, who gets hit by a vehicle after Monica whoo-whoo's at him on the street.

Everyone wants young, hip parents except for those who have them. Chandler's mom is a blond bombshell who is not only prettier than most of the women the male Friends date but also more successful and funnier.

No one could really blame any of Chandler's buddies for falling for her and putting a little twist on the Oedipus "he killed his father and married his mother" Rex theme. But by the same token, who can blame Chandler for being grossed out that his best friend is sexually attracted to his *mom*? Ick.

Meanwhile, Monica and Phoebe are facing one of the common denominators that all female friends go through—falling for the same guy . . . who just happens to be in a coma that they're to blame for.

Women often build fantasies about men based on the first date or even a chance encounter. By caring for a guy who's a vegetable, Monica and Phoebe invent things about him that they want in their relationships with Non–Coma Guys.

They weren't as fortunate as Sandra Bullock in *While You Were Sleeping* (who ends up with the comatose guy's brother), though, 'cause he turns out to be just a regular guy who's not particularly interested in either one of them. So they spurn him, which is just as well, anyhow.

He's probably gay. I think he has a certain quality.

WHAT THEY SAY:	WHAT THEY MEAN:
"I think we should see other people."	"Ha, ha. I already am." (Phoebe)

RAECHELL'S SPELLINK IS GOODE

It's obvious that though Rachel is serious about wanting to better herself, she still hasn't mastered how to type. On her résumé she boasts about her great "compuper" skills. But not her ability to use spell check. Rachel's attempt at writing a tawdry romance novel is foiled by her spelling errors—heaving "beasts" and throbbing "pens"? Either she's kinkier than she looks or she needs to buy a few more letters from Vanna. . . .

THE LENO CONNECTION

Jay Leno appears as himself when he has Nora Bing as a guest on *The Tonight Show*. The gig was old hat because he also played himself on *Mad About You* in a dream sequence that Murray the Dog had about being famous.

*J*ennifer Aniston is more of an artist than a writer. At eleven, some of her work was displayed at New York's Metropolitan Museum of Art.

(Jim Smeal/Galella Ltd.)

"The One with Mrs. Bing" Quiz

1. What is the name of Mrs. Bing's latest novel?
    a. *Euphoria Unbound*
    b. *A Woman Undone*
    c. *Lovers Passion*

2. On which talk show does Mrs. Bing appear?
    a. *Late Show with David Letterman*
    b. *The Tonight Show with Jay Leno*
    c. *Late Night with Conan O'Brien*

3. Where does the gang meet Mrs. Bing for dinner?
    a. Mexican Village
    b. Iridium
    c. Fiorello's

4. What does Ross say before Mrs. Bing kisses him?
    a. "Oh, my God."
    b. "Mrs. Bing . . . we shouldn't do this."
    c. "Uh-oh."

5. Phoebe and Monica each bring Coma Guy a bunch of things. Match the gifts to the Friend.

Monica	Foot massager
Phoebe	Etch-A-Sketch
	Balloons
	Sweater

6. What is Mrs. Bing's formula for romance writing success?

7. What is Rachel's middle name?

8. Who bought Chandler his first box of condoms?
    a. His mom
    b. His dad
    c. Ross

9. What are Phoebe's name choices for the Coma Guy?
    a. Scott or Hercules
    b. Glen or Agamemnon
    c. Randy or Johan

10. Why does Phoebe want to buy yesterday's *Daily News*?

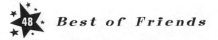

"THE ONE WITH MRS. BING" ANSWERS

1. a. *Euphoria Unbound*
2. b. *The Tonight Show with Jay Leno*
3. a. Mexican Village
4. c. "Uh-oh."
5. Phoebe and Monica each bring to Coma Guy:

Monica	Etch-A-Sketch
	Sweater
	Balloons
Phoebe	Foot massager

6. "Plug in half a dozen European cities and thirty euphemisms for male genitalia."
7. Karen
8. a. His mom
9. b. Glen or Agamemnon
10. She wants to know if her horoscope was right.

 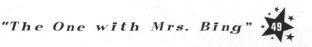

12. "The One with the Dozen Lasagnas"

****

Original air date: January 12, 1995

*E*veryone knows the sex of Ross's baby, except for Ross, who doesn't want to find out until it's born. Rachel's relationship with Paolo ends after he makes a pass at Phoebe. And though Monica hates him, she sends him off with one of the dozen lasagnas she made for her aunt, who doesn't want them anymore because they've got meat in them. Meanwhile, Chandler and Joey go shopping for a new kitchen table and come home with a Fooz ball table instead.

My friend Punky has this theory that unless you can eat it or wear it, animals aren't good for much else. While I'm not quite as vehement about that as she is, I do see her point.

Paolo has a cat. Paolo is a pig. Coincidence? I think not.

I don't trust men with cats. I also don't trust men with little dogs—they may as well be cats.

Though Paolo comes across as the strong, silent type, he's basically a weak, Italian slacker (just what does he *do*, anyhow?) who looks good in tight shirts and who travels to Italy a lot. He thinks he's so irresistible that Phoebe won't tell Rachel he put the moves on her. Nuh-uh.

Kudos to Rachel who does what many women wouldn't: She blames Paolo for putting Phoebe in an uncomfortable situation rather than wrongly accusing a friend of stealing her man. She's gotten savvier since the time she blamed Mindy for running off with Barry (see Chapter 2: "The One with the Sonogram at the End").

P.S. Ross finds out, so I think it's fair to blab: It's a boy!!!!

HEY, MON

By now it's become clear that the Friends have abbreviated nick-names for the women: Phoebe is Feebs (or Pheebs, if you want to be phonetically correct), Monica is Mon, and Rachel is Rach. But Chandler, Joey, and Ross are Chandler, Joey, and Ross. Why not Chan, Joe, and Rrrr? Joey does refer to Chandler as "Chan" once (in Chapter 24: "The One Where Rachel Finds Out"), but *only* once.

WHAT THEY SAY:	WHAT THEY MEAN:
"We should do this again."	"You will never see me naked." (Monica)

"THE ONE WITH THE DOZEN LASAGNAS" QUIZ

1. What TV show's theme song is the gang humming at the start of this episode?
   a. *The Odd Couple*
   b. *I Dream of Jeannie*
   c. *Batman*

2. Where were Rachel and Paolo going to go for their first away-trip together?
   a. Poconos
   b. Rome
   c. San Francisco

3. Paolo made a pass at Phoebe in Monica's living room.
   True   False

4. What do Phoebe and Rachel call Paolo?
   a. The cheating stud
   b. Pig Man
   c. Lying ingrate

5. What do Chandler and Joey call Ross?
   a. Anti-Paolo
   b. Milquetoast
   c. Sensitive Guy

6. When Ross comforts Rachel after her breakup, what does she say to him?
   a. "Why can't I fall in love with someone like you?"
   b. "What's wrong with me?"
   c. "I'm so sick of guys."

"**M**on," "Rach," and "Pheebs" smile pretty for the
birdie. (Janet Gough/Celebrity Photo Agency)

7. Who accidentally tells Ross the sex of his child?
   a. Carol
   b. Chandler
   c. Rachel

8. Ross says, "I want a daughter who'll adore me the way her mother
   doesn't."
   True   False

9. What are Monica's parting words to Paolo?
   a. "Don't show your face around here anymore, Pizza Boy."
   b. "Heat it at 375 until the cheese bubbles."
   c. "I don't like you at all, but I have one question: Why did you pick
   Rachel over me?"

10. What does Joey throw on his kitchen table that makes it collapse?
    a. A pan of lasagna
    b. A set of keys
    c. A skin magazine

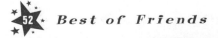

"THE ONE WITH THE DOZEN LASAGNAS" ANSWERS

1. a. *The Odd Couple.* Ross starts to hum *I Dream of Jeannie* afterward, but the gang quickly shushes him.

2. a. Poconos

3. False. He fondles her legs and rear end while she's giving him a massage at her massage clinic.

4. b. Pig Man

5. a. Anti-Paolo

6. c. "I'm so sick of guys."

7. c. Rachel

8. False

9. b. "Heat it at 375 until the cheese bubbles." (She gave him a pan of lasagna, remember?)

10. b. A set of keys

 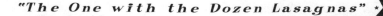

13. "The One with the Boobies"

Original air date: January 19, 1995

After Chandler accidentally sees Rachel wandering around topless after her shower, a chain reaction of nudity ensues when she tries to even the score by seeing his pee-pee. Joey finds himself playing the parent when he has to decide whether to hide his father's affair from his mom. And no one can stand Phoebe's latest boyfriend, an irritating psychiatrist named Roger.

It's obvious why Phoebe's with Roger. She's trying to find another David (flashback to Chapter 10: "The One with the Monkey," if you've forgotten who he is). While it's definitely undeniable that Roger is smart, he is also annoying, a busybody, and an uggo. I take Rachel's rave to Phoebe ("He's so cute") with a grain of salt. I've lied to many of my friends. The truth is usually saved till after the breakup.

The breakup between Phoebe and Roger is kind of like the debate about the chicken and the egg. Did she break up with him because the Friends wanted her to, or did the Friends want her to break up with him because they knew she wasn't happy with him? Maybe it's a little bit of both.

*I*n order to elicit the appropriate reaction, Jennifer Aniston apparently flashed her nippular area to Matthew Perry when they shot their boobie scene. No word on if anyone caught sight of his pee-pee.
(Janet Gough/Celebrity Photo Agency)

Roger points out some truisms about the Friends: that Chandler uses his humor to keep people at a distance; that they exude a dysfunctional group dynamic; that Ross feels guilty for being the Gellers' favorite child; that Monica equates food with love; and that in many ways the Friends are emotionally stunted.

And his point is?

CLUE PATROL

As far as I'm concerned, they all get what they deserve for being *stupid*. They leave their doors open? In *New York*? Uh, they might as well wear a sign that says: HI. ROB ME! Rachel gets extra dunce marks for prancing around naked in the living room—which has a big wide window and no shades. Then, too, there's that creepy Mr. Heckles living in the apartment building. I don't think it's beyond him to wander in one day, help himself to something in the fridge, sneak a peek at the girls (maybe the boys—we don't know about him yet), and then leave.

TALK THE TALK

"That's a relatively open weave and I can still see your nippular area."

—Chandler to Rachel, who's covering herself with a blanket

"THE ONE WITH THE BOOBIES" QUIZ

1. What type of blanket does Rachel use to cover up her chest from Chandler's view?
a. Old, holey comforter
b. Old, crocheted afghan
c. Old, knitted bed cover

2. Which Friends see one another naked in the shower?

3. Phoebe used to date someone called the Puppet Guy.
True   False

4. What does Chandler call Roger?
a. Fisher
b. Sparky
c. Shrink Guy

5. What does Mr. Tribbiani's mistress do for a living?

6. What is Mr. Tribbiani's vocation?

7. Why does Chandler call Joey Kicky?
   a. Because Joey was a top-rated soccer player in high school
   b. Because Kicky is the name of the character Joey plays in an Off-Broadway production
   c. Because Joey kicks in bed

8. Mrs. Tribbiani wishes her husband looked like Ralph Nader.
   True   False

9. Phoebe breaks up with Roger in Monica's apartment.
   True   False

10. When Mr. Tribbiani's mistress, Ronni, meets Joey for the first time, what's the first thing she offers him?
    a. Cheez-Nip
    b. An apology
    c. A good time

"THE ONE WITH THE BOOBIES" ANSWERS

1. b. Old, crocheted afghan

2. Rachel spies on Joey, thinking he's Chandler. Joey retaliates, but ends up seeing Monica, not Rachel. And Monica sets out to even the score with Joey, but ends up ogling Mr. Tribbiani instead.

3. True

4. b. Sparky

5. Ronni is a pet mortician.

6. He owns a pipe-fitting business.

7. c. Because Joey kicks in bed.

8. False. She wishes he looked like Sting.

9. False. She breaks up with him in Central Perk.

10. a. Cheez-Nip

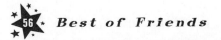

14. "The One with the Candy Hearts"

★★

Original air date: February 9, 1995

*R*oss's first date in nine years is on Valentine's Day with a beautiful neighbor. Susan and Carol, also out on a romantic date, end up at the same restaurant. Joey sets Chandler up on a blind date—with Janice. And Phoebe, Rachel, and Monica decide to spend the holiday building a Boyfriend Bonfire in their apartment.

The little lady wins a unanimous decision in round three of the bout between Chandler vs. Janice. After being heartlessly dumped twice in the past five months, Janice gets the last laugh—and it's an annoying one—this time around.

Chandler expects Janice to cry and cause a scene when he breaks up with her *again*. But she just smiles knowingly and says, "You can't live without me. And you know it. You just don't *know* you know it."

All he can counter with is, "Call me!"

The relationship between Chandler and Janice is a classic example of human nature. Because she adores him, always makes herself available to him, and constantly dotes on him, he doesn't want her. Compare this to how nuts Chandler gets in "The One with the Evil Orthodontist" when a woman won't acknowledge his phone calls. He wants her *more*.

As annoying as Janice's laugh is, she's a good soul who one day will make a good wife and, I suspect, an even better mother. Janice finally catches on that giving doesn't mean anything if the recipient doesn't want the gift.

My advice to her is one that's been passed down from mothers to daughters over the centuries: Say no once in a while and stay home and *really* wash your hair.

The dippiest Friend is played by the actress with the most prestigious education. Lisa Kudrow is a graduate of Vassar and has never participated in a Boyfriend Bonfire in real life. (Roger Dong/Outline)

As for Ross, it's great that he's getting back into circulation. Nine years is a long time. And even though most men would die to go out with a gorgeous woman like Kristen, it's understandable why he's not having a good first date with her. He's nervous, he's trying to impress her, and then his lesbian ex-wife with whom he's still in love shows up at the same restaurant with her life partner.

But things are looking up for Ross. After sharing a platonic-for-her/hopeful-for-him kiss with Carol, Ross rebounds fairly quickly when he sees another beautiful woman sashay past him.

The guy's depressed, but he's not dead.

TALK THE TALK

"You can go out with a creepy guy any night of the year.
I know I do."

—Monica, after Phoebe tells her she might go out with
Roger the Shrink on V-Day

———

"The Rachel thing's not working; your ex-wife is a lesbian.
I don't think we need a third."

—Chandler, giving Ross reasons to ask Kristen out

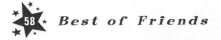

HE SAID/SHE SAID

"Having watched my father's career over the years, I'm not naive enough to think that good acting and writing is all it takes to have a hit show. There are so many factors that are relevant to which shows stay on the air and which ones don't."

—Matthew Perry, who has been in his share of duds

A barely-out-of-his-teens Matthew Perry in 1990. (Jim Smeal/Galella Ltd.)

"THE ONE WITH THE CANDY HEARTS" QUIZ

1. According to Janice, what does Chandler call out to her like?
   a. A tomcat
   b. A foghorn
   c. Church bells

2. Janice gives Chandler a bag of candy hearts that she had made up special. What do they say?

3. Carol is an anthropologist.
   True   False

4. Chandler orders two drinks at dinner with Janice. What are they?
   a. A martini, shaken, not stirred, and a Diet Coke
   b. A chocolate milk shake and a strawberry daiquiri
   c. Champagne and a Rob Roy

5. How did Ross and Kristen meet?
   a. At Lamaze class
   b. He borrowed an egg from her once
   c. In their apartment building's laundry room

6. In which restaurant do Ross and Kristen run into Carol and Susan?

7. While on his "blind date" with Janice, what does Chandler call the waiter?
a. Good Woman
b. Serving Boy
c. Excuse me, sir

8. For the girls' Boyfriend Bonfire, what do they need that they don't have?

9. When Chandler's about to dump Janice *again*, he says: "In my next life I'm coming back as _____."
a. A toilet brush
b. A canker sore
c. A pregnant woman

10. What has Janice done with all the pictures of her and Chandler?
a. Cut his head out of all the pictures
b. Framed them all
c. Mailed them to Chandler's former girlfriend

"THE ONE WITH THE CANDY HEARTS" ANSWERS

1. b. A foghorn

2. Chan and Jan 4-ever

3. False. Carol teaches sixth grade.

4. c. Champagne and a Rob Roy

5. b. He borrowed an egg from her once

6. Benihana's of Tokyo

7. a. Good Woman

8. The semen of a righteous man

9. a. A toilet brush

10. a. Cut his head out of all the pictures

15. "The One with the Stoned Guy"

****

Original air date: February 9, 1995

*A*fter working as a data processing permanent temp for five years, Chandler gets promoted to data processing supervisor, then quits. Ross has a date with a beautiful colleague named Celia and gives new meaning to the term "spanking the monkey," when he brings her back to his place to meet Marcel. Celia wants to meet his pee-pee, but only if he'll talk dirty to her. Meanwhile, Monica cooks a gourmet meal for a restaurateur looking for a new chef. Unfortunately, he's stoned and would just as well eat taco shells as her haute cuisine.

Déjà view, anyone? This show wreaks of *Seinfeld* influences, from the talk-dirty-to-me plot right down to Ross's utterance of *vulva* when he can't come up with anything dirtier. (Remember when Jerry Seinfeld couldn't remember the name of his girlfriend? All he could remember was that it rhymed with a part of a woman's anatomy, so he called her Mulva.)

It's nice to see that Ross isn't a basket case anymore and that he's doing well romantically. Actually, he's moving a lot faster than most people do after breaking up with a spouse. Of course, he has the added convenience of working with incredibly attractive women who want to date him.

Chandler is forced to grow up, too. Though he seems to me to be too much of a screwup for *any* company to want him so badly that they'd throw in incredible perks to get him to stay, he must know his stuff. While he enjoyed being a relative slacker at work, he's now become Boss Man Bing and is responsible for overseeing his former colleagues (See Chapter 22: "The One with the Ick Factor")—a touchy situation for a guy who likes to be liked.

He is about to join the ranks of the Suity Men he always mocks.

THE LOVITZ CONNECTION

Jon Lovitz played an important role in Lisa Kudrow's decision to become an actress. After graduating from Vassar with a B.S. in biology, Kudrow began doing research with her father, who is a headache specialist (curing, not causing). One of her brother's friends—Lovitz—told her she had what it took to become a great performer. With his encouragement, she joined the Groundlings improv group in L.A., and her career was launched.

Since leaving *Saturday Night Live,* Lovitz hasn't had any major acting coups. But his appearance as the stoned restaurateur on *Friends* won him rave reviews. He also got high visibility when he co-hosted the *MTV Movie Awards* with Courteney Cox in June 1995.

"THE ONE WITH THE STONED GUY" QUIZ

1. What does WENUS stand for?

2. Which Friend asks, "Can you see my nipples through this shirt?"

3. How much does Monica end up paying Rachel to waitress for her?
a. $10/hour
b. $15/hour
c. $20/hour

4. What is the name of Chandler's secretary?
a. Marsha
b. Helen
c. Steve

5. What does the restaurateur smoke prior to dinner at Monica's?
a. A cigar
b. A cigarette
c. A doobie

6. How many hours does Chandler spend on his career aptitude test?

7. Chandler has a rubber duck on his desk.
True   False

8. Chandler worked for seven years as a temp before getting promoted to data processing supervisor.
True   False

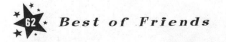

9. Ross says he's become the James Michener of talking dirty.
True   False

10. How does Joey help Ross get another date with Celia?
a. Joey practices talking dirty with Ross.
b. He helps Ross sweet talk her.
c. He offers to go out with her homely roommate so the four of them can double date.

"THE ONE WITH THE STONED GUY" ANSWERS

1. WENUS stands for Weekly Estimated Net Use of the System. It's a data processing term used at Chandler's office.

2. Chandler

3. c. $20/hour

4. b. Helen

5. c. A doobie

6. 8.5 hours

7. True

8. False. Chandler worked for five years as a temp before getting promoted.

9. True

10. a. Joey practices talking dirty with Ross.

*M*rs. Geller would not have approved of Courteney Cox's unruly 'do. But the audience at the *1995 MTV Movie Awards* ate it up.
(Jim Smeal/Galella Ltd.)

16. "The One with Two Parts (Part I)"

★★

Original air date: February 23, 1995

*J*oey *falls for Phoebe's twin sister, Ursula (who's moonlighting from Mad About You), making Phoebe feel neglected. Meanwhile, Chandler finds himself between a rock and a Bookbinder—Nina Bookbinder, that is—when he is told to fire her. And Ross has doubts about parenthood when he attends Lamaze classes with Carol and Susan.*

This episode illustrates the weirdness of dating a friend's sibling. When the relationship breaks up, as it will, you may have lost not only a girlfriend/boyfriend, but also a good friend.

Joey, of course, doesn't realize this when he decides to date Ursula. But he learns at the end just how precious Phoebe is to him. Joey may have starred in a Way-off-Broadway production of *Freud!*, but he has no clue that his attraction to Ursula may actually be his id telling his ego that he's got the hots for Phoebe. Think about it. It's so possible.

I think there's a potential plot line here about infatuation between Joey and Phoebe (though it should never reach fruition—can you imagine the loopy children these two would have?). Though Joey's the least developed character on *Friends,* the writers are finally making him less cartoonish by letting him feel real emotions instead of just portraying him as a walking hornfest.

NAME GAME

Jennifer Grant (daughter of Cary Grant and Dyan Cannon) plays Chandler's employee Nina, but in the credits she's listed as Michelle. There is a Michele (not a Michelle) on this episode, but it's an actress's name, not the name of a character. Michele Lamar Richards (who played Whitney Houston's jealous older sis in *The Bodyguard*) plays Carol's Lamaze instructor.

MY FRIENDS

"I try to never miss Friends *because it's such a fun show. Even though it stars all these young kids, I can relate to their lives. Everyone can, which is why I think the show is such a success."*

—Comedic writer Carl Reiner, who created the ultimate sitcom
The Dick Van Dyke Show

PATTY WHO?

On this episode about twins, it's no coincidence that the producers chose to have the Friends watch a clip from *The Patty Duke Show.* Courteney Cox, who says she's a *Munsters* gal herself, had no clue who Patty and Cathy—the twins Duke played on the classic sitcom—were. Maybe some youngster in the year 2025 will ask, "Who were Phoebe and Ursula?" Nah . . .

*P*heebs" and "Mon" are way more like sisters than "Pheebs" and her twin "Ursula." (John Paschal/Celebrity Photo Agency)

"THE ONE WITH TWO PARTS (PART I)" QUIZ

1. What's an ANUS? (Get your minds out of the gutters, kids.)

2. Who plays Ursula in this episode?
   a. Lisa Kudrow
   b. Helene Sherman
   c. Helene Kudrow

3. Ursula is Phoebe's only sibling.
   True   False

4. Who is Joey with when he meets Ursula for the first time?
   a. Phoebe
   b. Chandler
   c. His dad

5. When Chandler starts dating Nina, what does Ross tell him?
   a. "You don't dip your pen in the company ink."
   b. "That is not such a great idea."
   c. "Who's Nina?"

6. Who does Monica call "the little creature"?
   a. Mr. Heckles
   b. Marcel
   c. Paolo's cat

7. When Nina finds out Chandler told everyone he didn't fire her because she was cuckoo, she _____.

8. What does Phoebe want for her birthday?
   a. Her mom to be alive
   b. Bath salts
   c. A massage

9. Carol compares giving birth to passing a pot roast through a nostril.
   True   False

10. Which three shows do the Friends end up watching in Spanish?
    a. *Family Matters, Laverne and Shirley,* and *The Patty Duke Show*
    b. *The Patty Duke Show, The Dukes of Hazzard,* and *The Love Boat*
    c. *Family Ties, The Patty Duke Show,* and *Happy Days*

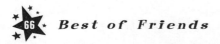

"THE ONE WITH TWO PARTS (PART I)" ANSWERS

1. ANUS stands for Annual Net Usage Statistics.

2. Technically either (a) Lisa Kudrow or (b) Helene Sherman is correct. While Kudrow plays both parts, her elder sister Sherman played the back of both characters' heads in over-the-shoulder shots.

3. False. They also have a brother. If you didn't get this right, it's okay. Ursula mentioned this on an episode of *Mad About You*.

4. b. Chandler

5. a. "You don't dip your pen in the company ink."

6. b. Marcel

7. Staples his hand

8. Either (a) Her mom to be alive, or (b) Bath salts is correct.

9. True

10. a. *Family Matters, Laverne and Shirley,* and *The Patty Duke Show*

 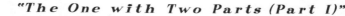

17. "The One with Two Parts (Part II)"

★ ★★★

Original air date: February 23, 1995

*A*fter *weeks of procrastinating, Rachel finally takes down the Christmas lights on their balcony, only to fall over and sprain her ankle. At the hospital, Rachel—who has no insurance—cajoles Monica into trading identities so she can use Monica's coverage. When Ursula breaks Joey's heart, Phoebe tries to fix it.*

Cox and Aniston prove to be excellent comedic actresses in "Part II," which is by far one of *the* best sitcom episodes ever, bar none. The verbal exchange between Monica pretending to be Rachel and Rachel pretending to be Monica is perfectly timed and hilarious. Lucy and Ethyl couldn't have done better.

The moral of this two-part episode, of course, is that lying is never the best policy, especially if you're basically an honest person. In "Part I," Chandler tries to get out of firing a beautiful employee by telling lies that backfire. By doing so, he loses a girlfriend. And Monica's and Rachel's lies make them seem schizoid to two really cute, really nice doctors who are interested in them.

The sweetest lie of all is when Phoebe pretends to be Ursula to make Joey feel better after the real Ursula pulls a Joey and dumps him without telling him why. There isn't any tonsil licking in their kiss but rather just pure, gentle emotion. Forget Ross and Rachel. *This* is the real odd couple.

MEDICAL CENTER

ER stars Noah Wyle and George Clooney guest-star as doctors who double date with Monica and Rachel. In another episode, Monica asks her ex-boyfriend Fun Bobby (Vincent Ventresca) to be her New Year's Eve date. Ventresca starred as the studly, sax-playing Dr. Tom Powell on

68

Fox's *Medicine Ball,* which was probably canceled because Dr. Powell's hair was too long. And Lauren Tom plays Ross's girlfriend in the series' 1995 season finale (just a few chapters away, kids). While Tom never appeared in a medical drama, she co-starred in *The Joy Luck Club* with Ming-Na Wen, who plays third-year medical student Deb Chen on *ER* opposite Clooney and Wyle.

"THE ONE WITH TWO PARTS (PART II)" QUIZ

1. Ugly Naked Guy is doing what in this episode?
   a. Hula hooping
   b. Playing with a Slinky
   c. Playing Scrabble with Ugly Naked Girl

2. What won't Phoebe eat?
   a. Monica's hummus
   b. Food with a face
   c. Chick peas

3. What does Joey give Phoebe for her birthday?
   a. Nothing
   b. A sweater from Bloomingdale's
   c. A Judy Jetson thermos

4. Dr. Mitchell and Dr. Rosen bring Monica and Rachel a bottle of wine from the cellars of Ernest and Tovah Borgnine.
   True   False

5. Monica has lived in her apartment for three years.
   True   False

6. When does Ross really feel like a dad?
   a. When Carol tells him he'll make a great father
   b. When Marcel grabs his index finger at the hospital
   c. When he begins to build a crib

7. What saves Rachel from being severly injured when she falls off the balcony?

8. What does Phoebe's birthday cake say?

9. Dr. Rosen treats Marcel at the hospital.
   True   False

10. The admissions nurse who is rude to Monica and Rachel is the same woman who was rude to Ross when he got hit in his face with a hockey puck.

True   False

"THE ONE WITH TWO PARTS (PART II)" ANSWERS

1. a. Hula hooping

2. b. Food with a face

3. a. Nothing

4. True

5. False. She's lived there for about six years.

6. b. When Marcel grabs his index finger at the hospital

7. Her leg gets tangled in a string of Christmas lights, which leaves her dangling outside of Mr. Heckles's apartment but prevents her from falling six floors to the ground.

8. "Happy Birthday Pee Hee." Ross dropped the cake and some of the letters merged into different configurations.

9. False. Dr. Mitchell treats Marcel.

10. False

*N*oah Wyle is buds with the Friends. Quite the little prankster, he (and fellow *ER* heartthrob George Clooney) defaced the Friends' dressing-room doors. But Courteney Cox doesn't seem to be holding a **grudge.** (Jim Smeal/Galella Ltd.)

18. "The One with All the Poker"

Original air date: March 2, 1995

*T*ired of being referred to by customers as "Excuse me," Rachel inter-
views for a job as an assistant buyer at Saks Fifth Avenue. She also sees
another side of the usually docile Ross when the girls face the boys during
a not-so-friendly game of poker. "I play to win," Ross tells Rachel. "If
you're going to play poker with me, don't expect me to be a nice guy."

Ross is actually on the right path to attracting Rachel's attention,
because at least on some level, most women are attracted to bad boys.
Being a *nice* guy who does nice things for her all the time has gotten him
nowhere. But when he plays poker, all of Ross's latent confidence comes
through.

In many ways, the way Ross taunts Rachel's novice poker-playing
skills is a classic boy-girl ritual. It's just the adult version of the little
boy pushing the little girl he likes in the schoolyard. Ross puts Rachel
down at the poker table, reveling in her frustration because he knows
that his ability is impressing her even though she won't admit it. At
poker, he is by far the best and gets overshadowed by no one—not even
by Chandler's wit or Joey's cheekbones.

Finally, the tension between Rachel and Ross is more equal.

POKER FACE

David Schwimmer is inadvertently responsible for this episode
being made. It was his idea for the cast members to bond by playing
poker together in real life. Though Courteney Cox and Matt LeBlanc sat
out because they didn't know enough about the game to play, they all
agreed that the experience was good for one and all. The writers thought
it was a good idea and wrote it into a script.

*M*att LeBlanc is a poker novice, but David Schwimmer is the *Friends* card shark.
(Janet Gough/Celebrity Photo Agency)

TALK THE TALK

> *"It's like the mother ship is calling you home."*

—Phoebe to Rachel, after the latter gets a job interview as an assistant buyer for Saks

"THE ONE WITH ALL THE POKER" QUIZ

1. Who teaches the girls how to play poker?

2. What song does Marcel keep listening to on Ross's CD player?
a. "Theme to The Monkees"
b. "The Lion Sleeps Tonight"
c. "Theme to Beauty and the Beast"

3. Which magazine does Rachel apply to?
a. *Popular Mechanics*
b. *Vogue*
c. *Reader's Digest*

4. Joey cried because he lost at poker.
True   False

5. At their last poker game, everyone is drinking a beer except for whom?

6. When Monica serves dainty hors d'oeuvres and crudités, Joey says food with more than one syllable can't be served at a card game. He suggests chips, dip, and what else?
   a. Pretz
   b. Dogs
   c. Pizz

7. What does Rachel call Ross when he bugs her?

8. Aunt Iris breaks the news to the girls that Tony Randall is dead.
   True   False

9. Rachel wins big time. What hand does she beat Ross with? (Hint: It's not right or left.)

10. Rachel thinks she's got an "in" with a job interviewer because she went to camp with:
    a. Her prospective boss, Barbara
    b. Barbara's cousin
    c. Barbara's husband

"THE ONE WITH ALL THE POKER" ANSWERS

1. Monica's Aunt Iris

2. b. "The Lion Sleeps Tonight"

3. a. *Popular Mechanics*

4. True

5. Ross. He's got a Snapple.

6. a. Pretz

7. Monkey Boy

8. True. Tony Randall fans take heart—he is *not* dead. Aunt Iris is trying to teach the girls how to pull off a good bluff.

9. Rachel wins with a full house.

10. b. Barbara's cousin

19. "The One Where the Monkey Gets Away"

★★

Original air date: March 9, 1995

*T*he gang frantically searches for Marcel, who slipped out of the apartment while Rachel baby-sat him. Meanwhile, Ross finally gets up the courage to try to woo Rachel. But just when it looks like the two might actually spend a romantic evening alone together, Barry, the ex–Mr. Potato Head, barges into the apartment declaring his love for her. "We have got to start locking that door," Ross says. Duh!

Okay, here's the poop. Marcel is a worthless little twit. Why? Because even though he's been with Ross for at least a couple of months now, his allegiance is to no one. When Ross, that creepy Mr. Heckles, and the gross Animal Control lady try to get Marcel to come to them, the stupid monkey vacillates and goes not to the person who has cleaned up his poop, fed him, and took him to bitchin' parties, but to the gal with the cage. *Hello?* You wouldn't find dogs like Eddie (*Frasier*) or Murray (*Mad About You*) betraying their owners.

Non sequitor: I think Ross gets so angry with Rachel not because she lost his monkey, but because she hasn't caught on yet that he likes her—and if she had, it would be that much easier for him because he wouldn't have to deal with telling her he really, really likes her.

The love triangle Rachel is caught in isn't one to die for. There's Ross, who can't bring himself to tell Rachel he's totally hot for her, and then there's nebbish Barry, who's having premarital jitters before getting hitched to Mindy.

Almost makes you wish Paolo were back, huh?

TALK THE TALK

"Hey, I don't need violence to enjoy a movie—just so long as there's a little nudity."

—Joey

*T*hough he's used to being photographed, Matt LeBlanc has been a serious photographer for the past ten years. (Albert Ortega/Galella Ltd.)

THE *GROWING PAINS* CONNECTION

Matthew Perry played Carol Seaver's boyfriend, Sandy, on *Growing Pains*. On the *Growing Pains* spin-off *Just the Ten of Us*, Matt LeBlanc played Murphy the quarterback, who *wanted* to be Wendy's boyfriend. There is no connection between Tracey Gold (Carol) and Brooke Thiessen (Wendy).

"THE ONE WHERE THE MONKEY GETS AWAY" QUIZ

1. At which eatery do Chandler, Ross, and Joey discuss Ross's infatuation with Rachel?
a. Joe-G Pizza
b. Riff's
c. Pontarelli's

2. Monica was in a high school production of *The Sound of Music*.
True   False

3. When Monica and Phoebe are searching for Marcel in the basement, what brushes up against Phoebe's right leg?

4. What apartment numbers do Monica and Rachel, and Joey and Chandler live in?
a. The girls live in Apt. 20. The boys in Apt. 19.
b. The girls live in Apt. 6. The boys in Apt. 7.
c. The girls live in Apt. 12. The boys in Apt. 13.

5. How does Louisa the Animal Control lady describe her old high school classmate Rachel during their school days?
    a. She says Rachel was the prettiest girl at Lincon High.
    b. She says Rachel was a bitch.
    c. She says Rachel was a slut.

6. Phoebe saves Marcel by pushing him out of the way of a tranquilizer pellet, which ends up hitting her in the butt. Which cheek gets shot?

7. Who inadvertently leads the gang to find Marcel in Mr. Heckles's apartment?
    a. Randy Man
    b. Ugly Naked Guy
    c. Banana Man

8. What outfit does Mr. Heckles have Marcel dressed in?
    a. A sailor's cap
    b. A pink tutu
    c. A diaper

9. Which one of the following wasn't one of Rachel's accomplishments in high school?
    a. Prom queen
    b. Homecoming queen
    c. Class vice president

10. Marcel poops in Monica's right shoe.
    True   False

"THE ONE WHERE THE MONKEY GETS AWAY" ANSWERS

1. a. Joe-G Pizza

2. True

3. Her left leg

4. a. The girls live in Apt. 20. The boys in Apt. 19.

5. b. She says Rachel was a bitch.

6. Right

7. c. Banana Man

8. b. A pink tutu

9. c. Class vice president. She was class president.

10. False. He poops in her left shoe.

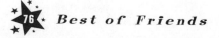

20. "The One with the Evil Orthodontist"

★★★

Original air date: April 6, 1995

*R*achel and Barry start dating again, which is kind of awkward 'cause he's now engaged to Mindy, who wants Rach to be her maid of honor. But when Rach finds out that Mindy and Barry had an affair while she was engaged to Barry, the two women decide to give Barry what for. Meanwhile, Chandler goes nuts when a woman he likes won't return his phone calls.

It's not that shocking that Rachel slept with her former fiancé. But it is surprising that Mindy will overlook Barry's history of cheating. She's so desperate for a doctor husband that she's willing to overlook a little complication like fidelity. Can you spell *looooooozer*? 'Cause that's what Dr. Farber and his soon-to-be missus both are.

A lot of guys would love to be in this picture. The Internet message board is loaded with fantasies about a "Courteney and Jennifer sandwich."
(John Paschal/Celebrity Photo Agency)

In any case, this is all good for Rachel. She's finally gotten him totally out of her system and can concentrate on dating men who aren't dating other women.

Chandler's situation with Danielle is so right on. His whole when-do-I-call-her dilemma is *insanely* true. It's nice to know that women aren't the only ones grappling with the when-do-I-call-back issue, though I suspect that more men are like Joey "Just stop calling her" Tribbiani than Chandler "Ring, dammit" Bing.

OPEN WIDE AND SAY AHHH

Mitchell Whitfield did such a good job playing Jennifer Aniston's ex-fiancé Barry the Orthodontist that he's playing another dentist on NBC's new sitcom *Minor Adjustment.* A couple other *Friends* co-stars are getting their own NBC shows, too. Jonathan Silverman (who delivers Carol's baby—see Chapter 23, "The One with the Birth") stars as a single guy in *The Single Guy.* His co-star, Jessica Hecht, will be pulling a Lisa Kudrow. Like Kudrow, who parlayed her co-starring role in *Mad About You* to a starring role in *Friends,* Hecht will continue to do guest spots as Susan on *Friends* while concentrating on *The Single Guy.*

THE MITCHELL CONNECTION

Mitchell Whitfield plays Dr. Barry Farber. George Clooney played Dr. Michael Mitchell three episodes ago. Coincidence or conspiracy?

"THE ONE WITH THE EVIL ORTHODONTIST" QUIZ

1. Which Friend cooks naked?

2. What treat does Barry buy for Rachel at Henri Bendel's?
a. Chanel perfume
b. A sexy Natori bra
c. A Vuitton wallet

3. Who does Phoebe out?

4. What does Rachel call Barry?
a. Molar Man
b. Satan in a Smock
c. Dr. Elton

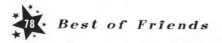

5. Who taught Rachel how to kiss?
   a. Barry
   b. Mindy
   c. Uncle Bob

6. Who does the Telescope Peeper turn out to be?
   a. Sydney Marx
   b. Mr. Heckles
   c. Ugly Naked Guy

7. Bernice is Barry's receptionist.
   True   False

8. After Rachel's tryst with Barry, what does Monica find in Rachel's hair?
   a. A pair of braces
   b. Dental floss
   c. A toothpick

9. How long does Chandler wait before calling Danielle?
   a. One hour
   b. One day
   c. One week

10. To whom does Telescope Peeper compare Monica?
    a. Ingrid Bergman
    b. Michelle Pfeiffer
    c. Courteney Cox

"THE ONE WITH THE EVIL ORTHODONTIST" ANSWERS

1. Joey

2. a. Chanel perfume

3. Mr. Peanut

4. b. Satan in a Smock

5. b. Mindy

6. a. Sydney Marx

7. True

8. b. Dental floss

9. b. One day

10. a. Ingrid Bergman

"The One with the Evil Orthodonist" **79**

21. "The One with the Fake Monica"

★★★

Original air date: April 27, 1995

*W*hen *Monica's credit card is stolen, she, along with Phoebe and Rachel, decide to catch the thief. Joey enlists his friends to help him come up with a less ethnic-sounding stage name. And when Ross finds out that Marcel has reached sexual maturity and needs to be with other monkeys, he tries to get him accepted into the Harvard of zoos.*

Now that Marcel's gone, none of the Friends have pets, which tells me that they have lives, that they haven't given up on finding a human partner, and that they take pride in their clothes (no cat hair on these kids). Ross seems like the type who might bring home a stray, but the fact that he's a Monkey Man proves he's more adventurous than even he would believe. But not nearly as adventurous as Fake Monica.

After Monica has her credit card ripped off, she finds herself envious of the woman who has taken over her identity, because Fake Monica is daring to live the life Monica has always dreamed about but was too chicken to try (I'm talking art classes and horseback riding here, not being a thief). Weirdness aside (like anyone actually would befriend their own personal thief), Monica—or Manana as she calls herself—gets to have the most fun she's had in ages before Fake Monica is caught and shipped off to Rikers Island.

Will Monica keep her *laissez-faire* attitude now that her little criminal buddy is locked away? Nope. She's a good girl and a big fat chicken at heart. And I'm kind of glad. If Monica let loose, there would be no thread to hold the rest of the loopy Friends together.

TALK THE TALK

"Why don't I just take off all my clothes and have a nightmare?"

—Monica to herself, when the tap instructor wants her to dance in
front of the class

———

"It's just something to do on the plane."

—Rachel to Marcel, after giving him the Curious George
doll he likes to hump

ALICIA WHO?

Before Alicia Silverstone became a bona fide movie star via the
hilarious film *Clueless*, she was best known as the girl in the Aerosmith
videos. But Silverstone isn't the first actress to garner tons of attention for
her work in a music video. Some ten years before Alicia ever stepped
foot on a video set, Courteney Cox was dancing with Bruce Springsteen
onstage in front of thousands of fans.

*M*atthew Perry, Jennifer Aniston, Lisa Kudrow,
and Courteney Cox attended the Pediatric AIDS Foundation benefit at the old
Robert Taylor Estate in Brentwood, California, on June 4, 1995.
(Albert Ortega/Celebrity Photo Agency)

"When I saw the world premiere of the ['Dancing in the Dark'] video on MTV, I waited and waited for my spots," Cox recalls. "I thought maybe they cut my scenes. Then when I finally appeared, I thought, 'That's it? Oh well.' But the response to that was so great. My agent was able to get me tested for parts by saying, 'Yeah, Courteney Cox—the girl who danced with Bruce—would be perfect for the role.'"

Cox, who claims to be a dorky dancer, gets to prove it in "The One with the Fake Monica," when she has to do a spazzy tap-dance routine. Bad job well done, Courteney.

"THE ONE WITH THE FAKE MONICA" QUIZ

1. What role does Joey read for in *Romeo and Juliet*?
a. Romeo
b. Mercutio
c. Tybalt

2. Which of the following is a stage name Joey doesn't consider?
a. Joseph Stalin
b. Holden Magroin
c. Chip Bestfield

3. When the girls find Fake Monica, what do they do?
a. Take her to lunch
b. Call the police
c. Make her pay Monica back

4. Marcel gets into San Diego Zoo.
True   False

5. Monica and Fake Monica go to the Big Apple Circus.
True   False

6. Joey decides to go by Flame Boy.
True   False

7. What going-away present does Phoebe give Marcel?
a. A poem she wrote for him to eat on the plane
b. A tin of homemade cookies
c. An aromatherapy kit

8. Monica paid $69.95 for a Wonder Mop.
True   False

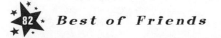

9. What does Phoebe call Marcel?

10. Joey auditions for *Cats*.
  True   False

"THE ONE WITH THE FAKE MONICA" ANSWERS

1. b. Mercutio

2. c. Chip Bestfield

3. a. Take her to lunch

4. True

5. False. They had planned to go.

6. False. Phoebe wants him to go by Flame Boy.

7. a. A poem she wrote for him to eat on the plane

8. True

9. Little Monkey Guy

10. False. Egged on by Fake Monica, Monica auditions for *Cats,* and gets out two syllables of "Memory" before being kicked off the stage.

 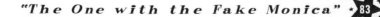

22. "The One with the Ick Factor"

✦✦✦

Original air date: May 4, 1995

*A*fter losing his virginity to her, Monica's boyfriend Young Ethan confesses that he's a high school senior. Rachel has erotic dreams about Joey and Chandler, making Ross both disgusted and envious. And when Phoebe temps as Chandler's secretary, she finds out that no one at work likes him anymore.

I don't think statutory rape is what people have in mind when they talk about older woman/younger man relationships. But that's what Monica unwittingly commits when she has sex with a guy who turns out to be a boy. They're both guilty of shaving four years off their ages, but in Monica's case, being twenty-two or twenty-six still makes her legal.

Rachel" has sweet dreams about the male Friends.
Is it any wonder why? (Janet Gough/Celebrity Photo Agency)

The funny thing is, until Ethan tells her how old he isn't, Monica doesn't have a clue. And though she admits she could've fallen in love with him, she breaks off the relationship faster than you can say "Buttafuoco." Good girl.

That Ross is jealous of Chandler and Joey having sex with Rachel in her subconscious is understandable, but he needn't worry. As Roger the Shrink would've told him, the people we dream about aren't necessarily the people we're really thinking of. Similarly, he shouldn't be that excited that she finally does dream about him. Now, if Rachel were *fantasizing* about Ross, then he'd have really something to celebrate.

WHAT THEY SAY:	WHAT THEY MEAN:
"You're such a nice guy."	"I'm going to be dating leather-wearing alcoholics and complaining about them *to* you." (Chandler)

COINCIDENCE?

If you list the Friends alphabetically by their real last names, you'll notice that all the actors were born in succession. Huh? Okay, Aniston was born in February, Cox was born in June . . . all the way down to Schwimmer, who was born in November. For exact birthdates, see Chapter 25: The One with the Cast Bios.

"THE ONE WITH THE ICK FACTOR" QUIZ

1. When Monica admits to Ethan she's not twenty-two, how old does she say she is?
a. Twenty-five and thirteen months
b. Twenty-six
c. Twentysomething

2. Why does Ross get a beeper?
a. So Carol can beep him when she goes into labor
b. So Rachel can beep him when she needs to talk to him
c. So the San Diego Zoo can contact him when Marcel gets lonely

3. What is the number of Ross's beeper?
a. 55JUMBO
b. 55JIMBO
c. 55BEEPS

4. In an attempt to get his employees to like him again, what does Chandler do?
   a. Buys lunch for everyone at Fiorello's
   b. Duets on "Ebony and Ivory" with a colleague
   c. Has a heart-to-heart with the guy who likes him the least

5. After his promotion, what do they call Chandler behind his back at the office?
   a. Boss Man Bing
   b. Bada Bing Bang Boom
   c. Mr. Bing

6. Monica wears a Reebok running outfit.
   True   False

7. Where does Rachel dream that she and Chandler have sex?

8. How long has Monica dated Ethan?

9. Rachel dreamed that Chandler and Joey had sex together.
   True   False

10. Why does Phoebe need a temp job?
    a. Because she's going to buy a car
    b. Because she taught a massage-yourself-at-home class and now they are
    c. Because she wants to take her grandma on a trip to Tibet

"THE ONE WITH THE ICK FACTOR" ANSWERS

1. a. Twenty-five and thirteen months

2. a. So Carol can beep him when she goes into labor

3. b. 55JIMBO

4. b. Duets on "Ebony and Ivory" with a colleague

5. a. Boss Man Bing

6. False. Monica wears a Nike running outfit.

7. On the Central Perk coffee table

8. Since mid-terms

9. True

10. b. Because she taught a massage-yourself-at-home class and they are

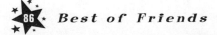

23. "The One with the Birth"

★ ★

Original air date: May 11, 1995

*W*hile Monica's biological clock ticks away like a time bomb, Carol goes into labor. When Ross and Susan can't stop bickering about who gets to help Carol more, Phoebe drags them into a closet to settle their differences—but all three end up getting locked in just as Carol's about to deliver the baby. Rachel flirts with an OB-GYN who has a love-hate relationship with women's private parts.

Phoebe's right. This little baby is one lucky guy. He has two moms, a dad, a doting aunt Monica, and a slew of surrogate aunts and uncles who are friends of his dad. That they were good friends and baby-sitters to Marcel (except for the Rachel incident when she temporarily lost him) proves that they genuinely care for Ross and most likely will make great caretakers for Baby Ben.

Expect Chandler and Joey to use the baby as a chick magnet. I think it would be too difficult for them *not* to take advantage of the adorable baby. But I predict that it will be Ross who attracts the most female attention when he takes the baby to the park, because it's always those who are the least conniving who profit the most.

I'm hoping Monica will hit the snooze button on her biological clock because the show does not need an unwed mother. And she has a proven track record of dating losers. Maybe when Young Ethan's all grown up, then they can hook up and create a stunning little human. But until then she should save her perfect eggs for something better.

KISS ME, KISS ME, KISS ME

Though none of the Friends are dating each other, they have shared smooches. Here's a tally:

*T*he youngest of ten siblings and step siblings, Courteney Cox—unlike Monica—is in no rush to have children of her own.
(Jim Smeal/Galella Ltd.)

Not surprisingly, Joey has kissed the most Friends so far. He shared a New Year's Eve lip lock with Chandler; mistakenly gave Phoebe a buss on the lips, thinking she was her twin, Ursula; and gave Ross a friendly peck on the cheek. For the record Joey not only kissed the real Ursula, but he also slept with her.

Rachel gave Ross a platonic kiss to thank him for teaching her how to do her own laundry on "The One with the East German Laundry Detergent." They also shared a soul kiss on "The One Where Rachel Finds Out," but that doesn't really count because it took place during a fantasy sequence.

While Ross never kissed Chandler, he *did* kiss Mrs. Bing after the two had a little too much to drink at dinner, which incited Chandler to call him a "mother kisser."

WHAT THEY SAY: WHAT THEY MEAN:

"It's not you."   "It's you." (Joey)

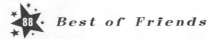

"The One with the Birth" Quiz

1. Why were Carol and Susan late to the hospital?
    a. They couldn't get a cab.
    b. Carol had a craving for hot dogs, so they went out to eat first.
    c. Susan had a craving for a Chunky and Carol wanted to look at stuffed animals first.

2. The doctor says Carol can consume only one thing prior to delivery. What?
    a. Ice chips
    b. Chunky
    c. A glass of lukewarm water

3. Besides Ross, who is the only other Friend who sees the delivery of the baby?

4. How do Carol and Ross and Susan decide on the name Ben for the baby?

5. Who does Ross say Ben looks like?
    a. Monica after a shower
    b. Uncle Ed covered in Jell-O
    c. Susan

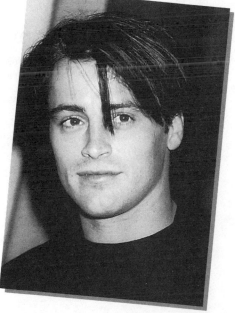

*M*att LeBlanc will be sporting dyed, blondish hair in the baseball-chimp flick, *Ed.*
(Miranda Shen/Celebrity Photo Agency)

 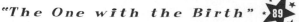

6. Which two of the following names were not in the running for the baby?

Jordy   Brandon
Jamie   Jesse
Cody   Dylan
Todd

7. Rachel's father is a doctor.
True   False

8. Chandler tells Monica that if neither of them are married by a certain age, they should have children together. At what age?
a. Forty
b. Forty-five
c. Never

9. Who gives Phoebe money *not* to sing in the hospital waiting room?
a. Ross
b. The admissions nurse
c. A pregnant lady

10. Joey is twenty-eight.
True   False

"THE ONE WITH THE BIRTH" ANSWERS

1. c. Susan had a craving for a Chunky and Carol wanted to look at stuffed animals first.

2. a. Ice chips

3. Phoebe. She's in the crawlspace above the delivery room.

4. From an old janitor's uniform Susan and Ross found in the closet when they're locked in.

5. b. Uncle Ed covered in Jell-O

6. Brandon and Todd

7. True

8. a. Forty

9. a. Ross

10. False. Joey is twenty-six.

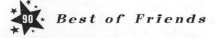

24. "The One Where Rachel Finds Out"

✦✦

Original air date: May 18, 1995

*A*fter eight months Rachel finally learns what we've known since day one. Ross is so in love with her. Monica is excited about becoming Friends-in-law with her roommate but gets defensive when Rachel can't decide whether she wants to be more than friends with Ross. But when she finally makes up her mind, it may be too late. He's with another woman with whom he's obviously romantically involved. And Joey's got his own love problem. His girlfriend wants to go to bed with him, but he can't yet. He's participating in a fertility study where he's making money hand over fist, if you know what I mean.

The real question here isn't, "How could Rachel not know Ross was in love with her?" but "How could Ross keep his crush a secret from Monica?"

Ross and Monica are pretty tight. He knows everything about her life and presumably confides in her. There is no way he wouldn't have thrown a few hints to Monica, if for no other reason than to feel out whether Rachel might talk about him when he's not there.

And Monica's no dummy—she definitely would've caught on about her brother's unrequited love for Rachel. Which means that both Phoebe and Rachel would've found out.

I also suspect that Rachel might have known all along that Ross had a crush on her. But since he never made it clear to her and she wasn't really interested, it was easier for her to ignore the whole issue than to deal with it.

Then, too, there's Ross, who in just a few days has struck up a relationship with Julie. It's not clear in this season finale whether Julie is a woman

he met in China, on the airplane, or perhaps is an old girlfriend with whom he's been reunited.

But no matter what happens in the future seasons, I've got to thank the writers for *not* ending the best sitcom of the decade with a lame-o romantic clinch between Ross and Rachel. This is real. And real life is always more interesting than fiction.

TALK THE TALK

"You think I'm going to tell a girl I like that I'm also seeing a cup?"

—Joey, on why he won't tell Melanie
he's participating in a fertility study

THE LAUREN CONNECTION

On the season finale, Ross was kissing his new girlfriend Julie (Lauren Tom). On *Family Ties*, Courteney Cox played a college psych major named Lauren who was dating Alex Keaton. Matthew Perry never played a character named Lauren, but he *did* play a snotty book editor named Alex on an episode of *Dream On*.

THE CHICAGO CONNECTION

Both Lauren Tom and David Schwimmer got their acting starts in Chicago. Tom was raised in the Windy City, while the Beverly Hills–bred Schwimmer attended Northwestern University (in the Chicago suburb of Evanston) and founded Chicago's Lookingglass Theatre Company.

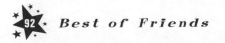

This may be stretching it, but so what? Tom is still remembered by cop-show fans as a kinky artist who liked to have sex in coffins (with live guys) on NBC's *Homicide*. And on ABC's *NYPD Blue* Schwimmer played a creepy, doomed apartment dweller who didn't have sex with anyone.

"THE ONE WHERE RACHEL FINDS OUT" QUIZ

1. Match the gifts Rachel receives to the proper giver:

Melanie	Cameo
Chandler	Fruit basket
Joey	Dr. Seuss book
Ross	Blouse (which she later exchanges for a skirt)
Monica	Travel Scrabble

2. While on a date with Rachel, who does Carl talk about?
a. His ex-wife
b. Ed Begley
c. Jodie Foster

3. How long has Ross been in love with Rachel?
a. Since ninth grade
b. Since she first moved in with Monica
c. Always

4. What does Monica call Joey?
a. Tiger
b. Pussycat
c. Wimp Boy

*C*ourteney Cox got her first big break playing Michael J. Fox's girlfriend in *Family Ties*. (Jim Smeal/Galella Ltd.)

5. Which Friend blabs that Ross is in love with Rachel?

6. How long was Ross in China?
   a. Three days
   b. One week
   c. A fortnight

7. Ross's new girlfriend has what color hair?
   a. Blond
   b. Black
   c. Auburn with golden flecks

8. How much is Joey making for participating in the fertility study for two weeks?
   a. $200
   b. $600
   c. $700

9. Ross gives Ben a good-bye kiss before he leaves for China.
   True   False

10. Why doesn't Ross hear Rachel calling out to him at the airport?

"THE ONE WHERE RACHEL FINDS OUT" ANSWERS

1. The gifts Rachel receives:

Melanie	Fruit basket
Chandler	Travel Scrabble
Joey	Dr. Seuss book
Ross	Cameo
Monica	Blouse (that she later exchanges for a skirt)

2. b. Ed Begley

3. a. Since ninth grade

4. a. Tiger

5. That'd be Chandler

6. b. One week

7. b. Black

8. c. $700

9. False. Ben appears only via photos in this episode.

10. He's got a pair of headphones on.

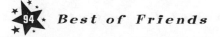

25. The One with the Cast Bios

★★

JENNIFER ANISTON

Born: February 11, 1969, in Sherman Oaks, California

Raised: A year in Greece; mostly in New York City

Current abode: Los Angeles

Famous relations: Dad John Aniston stars as Victor Kiriakis on NBC's *Days of Our Lives.* Godfather was the late Telly Savalas (who was Nicollette Sheridan's stepdad)

Nationality: Greek descent

Rah, rah, sis boom bah: Graduated from New York's High School of the Performing Arts in 1987. That's the *Fame* school.

Career notes: Off-Broadway roles in *For Dear Life* and *Dancing on Checker's Grave.* A blink and you'll miss her role in the feature film *Leprechaun.* A bigger role in her first post-*Friends* film, *Diary for an Insomniac.* TV parts on *Molloy, The Edge, Ferris Bueller, Herman's Head, Quantum Leap,* and *Burke's Law.* Aniston almost had to relinquish her role on *Friends* because she already was signed to CBS's *Muddling*

***R**ecognize her under all that bad hair? That's Jennifer Aniston hitting Spago's in Beverly Hills with pal Charlie Schlatter. (Jim Smeal/Galella Ltd.)*

Through. Luckily, the show sucked and got canned and she signed with *Friends.*

Nature: Loves outdoors—hiking, camping, and anything else dirt-related

Extracurricular activities: At eleven, Aniston had one of her paintings displayed at New York's Metropolitan Museum of Art.

Java choice: Mochaccino

Amour: Single

COURTENEY COX

Born: June 15, 1964, in Birmingham, Alabama

Current abode: Los Angeles

Famous relations: Fiancé Michael Keaton

Rah, rah, sis boom bah: Mount Vernon College, Washington, D.C. Dropped out after freshman year to model. Also took speech classes to lose her Southern accent

Career notes: Signed with Ford Modeling Agency's teen division and landed covers of Tiger Beat and teen romance novels. Also did commercials for Maybelline and Noxzema. Breakthrough role was dancing with the Boss in his video for "Dancing in the Dark." Landed gigs on *Another World, Family Ties, Misfits of Science, The Trouble with Larry, Murder, She Wrote, Seinfeld,* and *Dream On.* Also starred in the made-for-TV movies *Prize Pulitzer, Battling for Baby, Curiosity Kills* and *Till We Meet Again.* Her big-screen credits include *Ace Ventura: Pet Detective, Down Twisted, Masters of the Universe, Cocoon: The Return, Blue Desert, Shaking the Tree,* and *Mr. Destiny.* Starred onstage in *King of Hearts* at L.A.'s Tiffany Theater.

Hobbies: Likes riding motorcycles and swimming. Enjoys remodeling and decorating homes

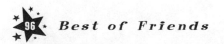

Java choice: Not. Courteney likes Lemon Soother Lipton tea (with honey).

Amour: Michael Keaton, man toy since 1990

LISA KUDROW

Born: July 30, 1963, in Encino, California

Current abode: Los Angeles

Famous relations: Former boyfriend Conan O'Brien and family friend Jon Lovitz

Rah, rah, sis boom bah: Vassar College in Poughkeepsie, New York, B.S. in biology

Career notes: Member of the Groundlings improv theater group. TV roles include *Mad About You* (which she's still on), *Bob, Cheers, Coach, Newhart,* and *Flying Blind.* The day after she was nominated for her first Emmy Award, Kudrow was back in the studio doing voiceovers for *Duckman.*

Extracurricular activities: She's a pool shark and an ace tennis player. She also performs with the Transformers improv group in her spare time.

Java choice: Not. Droste hot chocolate with a smidgen of whipped cream

Amour: Married to French ad-guy Michel Stern

MATT LeBLANC

Born: July 25, 1967, in Newton, Massachusetts

Current abode: Los Angeles

Famous relations: Nada

Nationality: His mom was born in Italy and he's often cast as Italian characters, but LeBlanc is also of Irish, French, English, and Dutch heritage.

Career notes: Best known for being an excellent human specimen in commercials for Levi's 501 jeans, Coca-Cola, Doritos, and Milky Way. The Heinz ketchup ad he starred in won the Gold Lion Award at the 1987 Cannes Film Festival. His TV roles include *TV 101, Just the Ten of Us, Vinnie & Bobby, Top of the Heap, Reform School Girls,* and *Red Shoe Diaries.* LeBlanc also played Robert "I dare you to knock this battery off my shoulder" Conrad's kid in 1990's made-for-TV flick *Anything to Survive.* He is also looking Italian on the big screen in *Lookin' Italian* and *Ed.*

Nature: Although the toothy one is used to being photographed, LeBlanc enjoys being on the other end of a camera. He's quite the shutterbug and specializes in landscape photography.

Extracurricular activities: Traveling to locales like Amsterdam, Germany, and Switzerland.

*E*ver since he got his first motorcycle at the ripe old age of eight, Matt LeBlanc has been consumed by the need for speed. Both he and *ER* pal, Anthony Edwards, got their ya-yas when they raced in the Toyota Grand Prix in Long Beach, California, in March 1995.
(Jim Smeal/Galella Ltd.)

Java choice: Café mocha

Amour: Like Hugh Grant, LeBlanc paid bucks for his lady (forty, to be exact) . . . only this Lady is a mutt he rescued from the dog pound.

MATTHEW PERRY

Born: August 19, 1969, in Williamstown, Massachusetts

Raised: Ottawa, Ontario, and Los Angeles

Current abode: Los Angeles

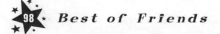

Famous relations: John Bennett Perry, the Old Spice guy, is his dad. Matthew said he used to hate bringing girlfriends home to meet his father because they inevitably fell for the handsome, elder Perry.

Rah, rah, sis boom bah: Perry's plans to matriculate at the University of Southern California were put on hold indefinitely when he got the lead role in the stinky sitcom *Boys Will Be Boys.*

Career notes: Perry was a regular on *Sydney* and *Home Free,* and a recurring guest star on *Growing Pains.* He also appeared on *Beverly Hills, 90210, Empty Nest, Who's the Boss, The Tracey Ullman Show,* and *Dream On.* His made-for-TV movie credits include *Deadly Relations, Dance 'til Dawn,* and *Call Me Anna.* On the big screen Matthew appeared in *A Night in the Life of Jimmy Reardon, Parallel Lives,* and *She's Out of Control.* In July 1995, Perry began filming 20th Century Fox's *Independence Day.*

Nature: He likes nature, if it involves playing hockey

Extracurricular activities: Perry is quite the little writer. In 1993 he sold a pilot for a series called *Maxwell's House* to Universal Television. Perry is also quite the athlete. Besides hockey and softball, he's an excellent tennis player and was nationally ranked in, well, Canada.

Java choice: Coffee with cream and two Equals

Amour: Single (!!!)

DAVID SCHWIMMER

Born: November 12, 1966, in Queens, New York

Raised: Los Angeles

Current abode: Los Angeles and Chicago

Famous relations: His attorney mom, Arlene, handled Roseanne's divorce from the guy who wasn't Tom Arnold.

The One with the Cast Bios

Rah, rah, sis boom bah: Beverly Hills High, where he was a theater jock, and Northwestern University in Evanston, Illinois. Schwimmer got his B.S. in speech/theater in 1988.

Career notes: Appeared in *Monty, NYPD Blue, Blossom, L.A. Law,* and *The Wonder Years.* His feature film credits include *Crossing the Bridge, Twenty Bucks,* and *Flight of the Intruder.* Schwimmer has acted in and directed numerous stage productions, including *West, The Odyssey, Of One Blood, In the Eye of the Beholder, The Master and Margarita, The Jungle, The Serpent,* and *Alice in Wonderland.*

Extracurricular activities: Cofounded Chicago's Lookingglass Theatre Company. His direction of *The Jungle* won six Joseph Jefferson Awards (Chicago's version of the Tonys). Also appears in AT&T commercials

Java choice: Double latté with skim milk

Amour: A Louisiana lawyer he's been dating since 1993

26. The One with All the Guest Stars

★★★★★★★★★★★★★★★★★★★★★★★★★★★★★★★★★★★★★★★

*E*ver wonder who all those peripheral people on *Friends* are? Some are famous (Jay Leno, Elliott Gould, George Clooney). Others aren't (Joel Gretsch, anyone?). Some (Mitchell Whitfield, Jonathan Silverman) got their own TV shows (Gee—you think it's a coincidence that the title of Silverman's new show—*The Single Guy*—sounds like it could be a character on *Friends*?). Others are happy to be recurring guest stars (Jane Sibbett). But each and every one of them makes *Friends* a better show. So here's to them:

Acovone, Jay (Fireman Charlie: One of the three cute firemen who put out the female Friends' Boyfriend Bonfire)

Armstrong, Jack (Bob: Joey's ex-girlfriend Angela's new boyfriend, whom Monica wants to date)

Azaria, Hank (David: Phoebe's physicist boyfriend)

Barone, Anita (Carol No. 1: Ross's ex-wife. Appeared in only one episode before being replaced. See Sibbett, Jane.)

Blaze, Tommy (Carl: Rachel's date, whom she leaves to go meet Ross at the airport)

Bohrer, Corinne (Melanie: Joey's girlfriend during the time he's donating sperm to an NYU fertility study)

Bryte, Leesa (Leslie: One of Rachel's rich buddies)

Buckner, Brian (One of Chandler's employees who mocks the way he speaks)

Burr, Fritzi (Mrs. Tedlock: Chandler's supervisor)

Cassaro, Nancy (Shelly: Chandler's colleague, who, believing he's gay, tries to set him up with another man)

Cavanagh, Megan (Louisa: A jealous high school classmate of Rachel and Monica's who works for Animal Control and intends to take Marcel away)

Caya, Benjamin (Bratty Boy who steals Ross's hockey puck in the hospital waiting room)

Clark, Lynn (Danielle: The woman Chandler thinks is blowing him off by not returning his calls)

Clooney, George (Dr. Michael Mitchell: One of the two docs who takes care of Rachel's sprained ankle. Also extracts Scrabble tiles from a choking Marcel)

Connick, Jill (Jill Goodacre: The Victoria's Secret model whom Chandler gets stuck with in the ATM vestibule. Note: Jill Connick *was* Jill Goodacre before she married Harry Connick, Jr.)

Costanzo, Robert (Joey Tribbiani Sr.: Joey's cheatin' dad)

Donahue, Elinor (Aunt Lillian: Monica and Ross's aunt)

Fairchild, Morgan (Nora Tyler Bing: Chandler's mom)

Fratkin, Stuart (Lowell: A gay colleague whom a fellow employee tries to set Chandler up with)

Fusco, Cosimo (Paolo: Rachel's Italian boyfriend)

Garland, Beverly (Aunt Iris: Monica and Ross's poker-playing aunt)

Garlington, Lee (Ronni: Mr. Tribbiani's mistress)

Gillingham, Kim (Angela: Joey's former girlfriend)

Gleason, Mary Pat (Nurse Sizemore: The mean nurse who accidentally gets hit with the same hockey puck that hit Ross in the face)

Gould, Elliott (Jack Geller: Monica and Ross's dad)

Grant, Beth (Lizzy the Homeless Woman: Phoebe gives her $1,000 and a football phone)

Grant, Jennifer (Nina: The woman Chandler has to fire but ends up dating instead)

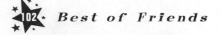

Gretsch, Joel (Fireman Charlie: One of the three cute firemen who put out the female Friends' Boyfriend Bonfire)

Grey, Jennifer (Mindy: Rachel's ex–maid of honor)

Hagan, Marianne (Joanne: One of Rachel's rich friends)

Hall, Alaina Reed (Admissions woman at the hospital where Rachel gets her sprained ankle treated)

Hankin, Larry (Mr. Heckles: The weird guy in the apartment building who claims other people's animals are his)

Hardin, Melora (Celia: Ross's girlfriend who likes it when he talks dirty to her)

Harris, Lara (Obsession Girl who worked with Joey at Macy's)

Hecht, Jessica (Susan: Carol's lover)

Hunt, Helen (Jamie: Central Perk customer visiting from *Mad About You.*)

Kenzle, Leila (Fran: Central Perk customer visiting from *Mad About You.*)

Kirsch, Stan (Ethan: Monica's jailbait boyfriend)

Klark, Kerrie (Flight representative who gives Rachel's message not to Ross, but to a married man)

Leno, Jay (Himself)

Lewis, Clea (Franny: Monica's colleague who also slept with Paul the Wine Guy)

Lewis, Jennifer (Paula: Monica's colleague at work)

Lovitz, Jon (Steve: The stoned restaurateur who wolfs down Monica's gourmet meal)

Lower, Geoffrey (Alan: Monica's boyfriend that everyone except she is in love with)

Lowery, Carolyn (Andrea: A guest at Nana's funeral who flirts with Chandler until her friend tells her he's gay)

MacDonnell, Sarah (Sandy: Joey's New Year's Eve date who brings her two children to Monica's party)

Maika, Michele (Kiki: One of Rachel's rich friends)

Mann, Cynthia (Jasmine: Phoebe's colleague)

Markoe, Merrill (Marsha: Ross's colleague)

Medway, Heather (Kristen: Ross's Valentine's Day date)

Milos, Sofia (Aurora: Chandler's dream woman who won't commit to just one man)

Miranda, Christopher (Bobby: Kid getting his teeth fixed while Rachel returns her engagement ring to Barry)

Nelson, John Allen (Paul the Wine Guy: Monica's date)

Pagano, Jo Jean (Cranky cappuccino customer at Central Perk)

Pickles, Christina (Judy Geller: Monica and Ross's mom)

Poindexter, Larry (Fireman Dave: One of the three cute firemen who put out the female Friends' Boyfriend Bonfire)

Pringle, Joan (Dr. Oberman: Carol's OB-GYN)

Remini, Leah (An unwed woman whose baby Joey helps deliver)

Richards, Michele Lamar (Carol, Ross, and Susan's Lamaze instructor)

Saviola, Camille (Horrible woman in Laundromat who gives Rachel a hard time during her first laundry outing)

Sederholm, David (Coma Guy: The cute guy who gets hit by a car after Monica "whoo-whoos" at him)

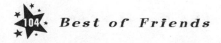

Shear, Claudia (Fake Monica: The woman who stole Monica's credit card)

Shearer, Harry (Dr. Baldkara: An unscrupulous man who tries to buy Marcel to fight with other animals)

Sibbett, Jane (Carol No. 2: Ross's ex-wife. See also Barone, Anita)

Sivad, Darryl (Employee who makes fun of the way Chandler speaks)

Silverman, Jonathan (The doc who delivers Carol's baby. Also the star of NBC's *Friends* ripoff sitcom, *The Single Guy.*)

Sjoli, Elisabeth (Tia: A beautiful neighbor Chandler and Joey meet when they're looking for Marcel. Roommates with Samantha)

Smith, Philip Rayburn (Actor auditioning for *Romeo and Juliet*)

Stevens, Fisher (Roger: Phoebe's creepy shrink boyfriend)

Tamburrelli, Karla (Monica and Fake Monica's tap teacher)

Tokuda, Marilyn (Nana's nurse)

Tom, Lauren (Julie: Ross's girlfriend)

Vaccaro, Brenda (Gloria Tribbiani: Joey's mom)

Valen, Nancy (Lorraine: Joey's pre–Valentine's Day date who's fond of eating chocolate mousse off men)

Ventresca, Vincent (Fun Bobby: Monica's ex-boyfriend)

Visser, Angela (Samantha: A beautiful neighbor Chandler and Joey meet when they're looking for Marcel. Roommates with Tia)

Whalen, Sean (The Pizza Guy who accidentally delivers George Stephanopoulos's pizza to the female Friends)

Wheeler, Maggie (Janice: Chandler's on-again, off-again girlfriend)

Whitfield, Mitchell (Barry: Rachel's ex-fiancé)

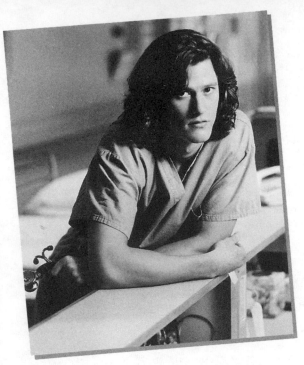

Wilson, Dorien (Mr. Douglas: Chandler's boss)

Wright, Max (Terry: Rachel's boss at Central Perk)

Wyle, Noah (Dr. Jeffrey Rosen: One of the doctors who consults on Rachel's sprained ankle)

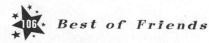

27. The One with the Loopy Lingo

★ ★

FRIENDSPEAK

So you wanna speak like the Friends, only you can't remember all their floopy terminology? Not to worry. It's so not hard.

Just add a *y* (pronounced "eee") at the end of the desired word, preferably a verb: "What's with that flippy thing with your hair?" And if you're talking about a person, add guy or girl to the description. For instance: "Talky Guy asked Itchy Girl out on a date."

Also, be sure to make liberal usage of *not* and *so*: "Do we not like them?" or "You are so going to Minsk." Use *so* and *not* together in the same sentence and get a double whammy: "That is so not true." Add emphasis to *not* and you've got Chandler: "That is so *not* true!"

To talk specifically like Chandler, remember to put emphasis on a word that normally wouldn't be emphasized, e.g.: "Could that report *be* any later?" or "The hills are alive with the sound *of* music." Also, let all your innate smartassness come out and say exactly what's on your mind, preferably with a smirk.

*L*isa Kudrow is *so* not dumb.
(John Paschal/Celebrity Photo Agency)

Add a "shall we" at the end of any sentence and you've become Monica: "Let's analyze this, shall we?"

If Ross is your speech god, just enunciate everything very clearly and make use of archaic terms: "I want to woo her." Sprinkle in plenty of non sequitors to be more like Pheebs. And if you wanna talk like Joey, be sure to state the obvious and then add, "if you know what I mean," at the end of the thought.

Friendspeak is so *not* hard, if you know what I mean. So let's all try it, shall we?

FRIENDISMS	REAL TALK
Doi	Duh
Filter tip, little buddy	Cigarette
Floopy	Messed up
Icky	Gross
Nippular area	Boobies
Nuh-uh	No way
So not true	Not true
Testosteroney	Macho
Um, no	No
Wee	Minute
Why so scrunchy?	Why are you such a crab?
Yuh-huh.	Oh, yeah

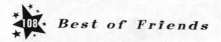

28. The One with the Rembrandts & the Creative Team

★ ★

I'll Be There for You" turned the Rembrandts into bona fide rock stars. (Michael Tighe)

THE REMBRANDTS

Phil Solem and Danny Wilde hooked up in 1976, around the same time that Monica Geller's boyfriend, Young Ethan, was conceived. Back then, they went by the band name of Great Buildings. These days they're known as the Rembrandts.

Though they've had a cult following since their 1990 single "That's Just the Way It Is Baby" hit the charts, the Rembrandts didn't become household names till they sang "I'll Be There for You," the theme to—you got it— *Friends.*

"[Producer] Kevin Bright liked 'That's Just the Way It Is Baby' and approached us about singing the theme to the show," said Wilde. "He wanted us to do kind of a retro-y thing. So he sent us the pilot and we thought it was kind of funny, so we said, 'Let's do it.' We went in for like twenty hours on a Saturday, got it done and then the show premiered later that week."

The peppy theme song, which doesn't sound like any of the band's more serious tunes, almost didn't make it on to *LP*, their third CD. But when radio stations began playing looped versions of the forty-two-second theme, the Rembrandts' record company suggested they record a full-length rendition for *LP*. But by the time the song made it on to the album, the sleeve had already been printed *without* "I'll Be There for You" on the jacket.

"There are about 250,000 records out there without the song credited on the album," Solem said. "We like to think of those as collector's items."

Making the video for the single proved to be another first for the band—they shared screen time with the six hottest actors on TV. Asked to dish the dirt on the gang, the Rembrandts came clean.

"We had heard that Courteney [could be a primadonna]," said Wilde.

Just tell us she was a bitch, okay?

"No, she was a sweetheart," said Wilde. "She was so cool. I love her."

Added Solem, "All those chicks are very hot. The video was really fun 'cause it was all scripted out, but once they got there it just flew out the window. They worked their own bits and it was a free-for-all. Danny and I played the Dean Martin role and they were Jerry Lewis. "

THE CREATIVE TEAM

Who: Producers David Crane, Marta Kauffman, and Kevin Bright.

What: Crane and Kauffman's previous gigs were creating *The Powers That Be* and *Family Album*. The pair, who've been writing partners for more than seventeen years, hooked up with Bright to create the Emmy Award–winning *Dream On*. Matthew Perry's guest-starring role as a power-hungry young editor on *Dream On* led to his being cast in *Friends*.

Their roles: Though all three are credited as producers, Crane and Kauffman primarily write the shows while Bright concentrates on casting and producing.

Casting: They admit that the chosen six weren't the only actors they auditioned. As many as five actors were considered for some of the roles. Originally they had wanted Courteney Cox for the part of Rachel, but Cox, who identified with Monica, fought for the role and won.

Little white lie: They claimed that whenever a sexual act was depicted, a condom wrapper would always be visible. Not to this eye.

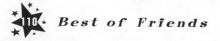

29. The One with the Really Long Quiz

★★★

QUIZARAMA

Now you're up to speed on what happened during the first season of *Friends*. And you've presumably caught them in some of their extracurricular activities and boned up on their earlier projects. Let's see if you're just pals or are best friends with the gang.

1. Who was the first to see the other naked?

2. Which Friend appeared as Eve's unwilling, handcuffed love slave on *Larroquette*?

3. What was the name of Monica and Ross's childhood dog?
   a. Spot
   b. Julio
   c. Chichi

4. Which of Joey's sisters has a restraining order on her?

5. What's the name of the softball team that the Friends finally beat?
   a. Hasidic Jewelers
   b. Central Perk Sluggers
   c. New York WENUS

6. How does Monica guestimate the size of men's penises?

Do you know where this man's **WENUS** is?
(John Paschal/Celebrity Photo Agency)

7. Where did the Rembrandts shoot their video for the *Friends* theme song "I'll Be There for You"?

8. When Courteney Cox introduced Val Kilmer at the *1995 MTV Movie Awards,* how did she introduce him?

a. "Here's the guy who took Batman away from my honey, Michael Keaton."

b. "Please welcome Batman—Val Kilmer."

c. "Everyone put their hands together for Mr. Val Kilmer."

9. What color are Monica's wine goblets?

10. How much did Rachel's parents spend on her wedding to Barry?

11. What can Phoebe do that the others can't?

a. She can sing all the words to the national anthem.

b. She can successfully cook a turkey in a microwave.

c. She can sleep in public places.

12. Courteney Cox played Michael J. Fox's girlfriend in *Family Ties.* What was her character's name? (I told you a few chapters ago, remember?)

13. Which Friend got bitten by a peacock at the zoo?

14. Phoebe is left-handed.
True   False

15. Ross sees a framed picture of Carol and Susan with their friend Tanya. What celebrity does he mistake Tanya for?
a. k.d. lang
b. Huey Lewis
c. Florence Henderson

16. What was the name of Chandler's roommate before Joey?
a. Angela
b. Kip
c. Brad

17. What kind of cookies does Phoebe make better than anyone else?
a. Oatmeal raisin
b. Chocolate-chunk macadamia
c. Peanut butter and marshmallow

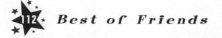

18. How old was Chandler when his parents divorced?

19. A gold frame frames the peephole on Monica's door.
    True　　　　False

20. How did Ross end up majoring in paleontology in college?
    a. On a dare
    b. Based on an aptitude test
    c. Carol was majoring in paleontology

21. What does Rachel call Chandler when he's smug?
    a. Sarcastic Boy
    b. Smirky
    c. Kicky

22. The Friends live in what part of New York?
    a. Brooklyn
    b. Tribeca
    c. Greenwich Village

23. Before admitting to Chandler that he kissed Mrs. Bing, who does Ross say kissed her?
    a. Paolo
    b. Joey
    c. The headwaiter

24. What is Ross's "nickname" for Paolo?

25. When Chandler was eleven, his mom wrote *Mistress Bitch*, which embarrassed him tremendously.
    True　　　　False

26. Encouraged to write by Mrs. Bing, Rachel begins to write a book called _____.

27. Monica and Rachel live on what floor?

28. Monica once served Phoebe goose pâté but told her it was vegetarian.
    True　　　　False

29. In what episode does Chandler first bring up the game Kerplunk?
    a. "The One with All the Poker"
    b. "The One with the Boobies"
    c. "The One with the Monkey"

The One with the Really Long Quiz

30. Matthew Perry played Tracey Gold's boyfriend on *Growing Pains*. What was his character's name?
a. Sandy
b. Ben
c. Robin

31. Who directed the Rembrandts' video for "I'll Be There for You"?
a. Sean Alquist
b. Marcel
c. Herb Ritts

32. Who is the only cast member who *doesn't* smoke?

33. On what sitcom did Matthew Perry make his TV debut?
a. *Boys Will Be Boys*
b. *Second Chance*
c. *Charles in Charge*

34. Which female Friend was hired and then fired to play Roz on the pilot for *Frazier*?

35. After co-hosting the *1995 MTV Movie Awards*, which celebrity was Courteney Cox linked with?
a. Chris Isaak
b. Val Kilmer
c. Jim Carrey

36. When she was eight, Ursula broke Phoebe's Judy Jetson thermos by throwing it under a bus.
True   False

37. Marcel almost chokes to death on the thimble piece from Monopoly.
True   False

38. Rachel went to boarding school.
True   False

39. Ugly Naked Guy has a pair of gravity boots.
True   False

40. Which Friends' bedrooms have we not seen yet?

41. When Joey borrows money from Chandler, how much does Chandler say Joey owes him?
a. 10 bucks
b. $100,000
c. 17 jillion dollars

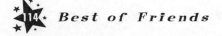

*L*ike Harrison Ford, Matt LeBlanc worked as a carpenter before switching over to acting. (Jim Smeal/Galella Ltd.)

42. Joey takes classes at NYU.
True   False

43. Joey's girlfriend, Melanie, works at Laundorama.
True   False

44. Why does Ross go to China?
a. To participate in an archaeological dig
b. To convince the Chinese government to allow an artifact to be brought to the U.S.
c. To curate a museum in Beijing

45. Who does Ross give a photo of himself to?
a. Rachel
b. Carol
c. Monica

46. Where did Rachel meet Carl, the Ed Begley–obsessed guy?

47. What did Ross buy for Rachel when he fell in love with her in college?
a. A set of *Cliffs Notes*
b. A crystal duck
c. A mood ring

48. Joey worked as the _____ Guy at Macy's.
a. Aramis
b. Obsession
c. Armani

49. Joey has six brothers and sisters.

True   False

50. Coma Guy gets hit by a milk truck.

True   False

QUIZARAMA ANSWERS

1. Chandler. He saw Rachel's "nippular area" when she came out of the shower. (In "The One with the Thumb," it's alluded to that Rachel and Phoebe *might* have seen Little Joey when Joey, wearing just a robe, sits open-legged on Monica's sofa. But there's no confirmation of a pee-pee sighting in this episode.)

2. Matthew Perry. He played Steven.

3. c. Chichi

4. Joey's little sister Tina's husband puts a restraining order on her. Why? I don't know.

5. a. Hasidic Jewelers

6. The distance from the tip of a guy's thumb to the tip of his index finger

7. NBC's Studio 8H in New York City, where *Saturday Night Live* tapes its shows

8. b. "Please welcome Batman—Val Kilmer."

9. Blue

10. $40,000

11. c. She can sleep in public places.

12. Lauren

13. Chandler

14. True

15. b. Huey Lewis

16. b. Kip

17. a. Oatmeal raisin

18. Nine

19. True

20. a. On a dare

21. b. Smirky

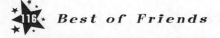

22. c. Greenwich Village

23. a. Paolo

24. Ross calls Paolo "Rigatoni."

25. True

26. *A Woman Undone*

27. The sixth floor

28. True

29. b. "The One with the Boobies"

30. a. Sandy

31. a. Sean Alquist

32. David Schwimmer

33. c. *Charles in Charge*

34. Lisa Kudrow

35. a. Chris Isaak. He denies it.

36. True

37. False. He chokes on a Scrabble tile.

38. False. Chandler went to boarding school.

39. True

40. Rachel, Phoebe, and Ross

41. c. 17 jillion dollars

42. False. Joey participates in a fertility study at NYU Medical School.

43. False. Melanie works at The Three Basketeers.

44. b. To convince the Chinese government to allow an artifact to be brought to the U.S.

45. c. Monica. Ross wants her to show Ben his picture so that the baby doesn't forget him while he's in China.

46. At Central Perk

47. b. A crystal duck

48. a. Aramis

49. True

50. False. Coma Guy gets hits by an ambulance.

DID YOU KNOW THAT . . . ?

Ross and Rachel do their first load of laundry together at Laundorama.

Chandler's preferred Thanksgiving meal is tomato soup, grilled cheese sandwiches, and a large bag of Funions.

Rachel was just $100 short when she wanted to buy a plane ticket to Vail to go skiing with her folks.

Ross lent Carol a skull for one of her classes.

Susan and Carol refer to Ross as Bobo the Sperm Guy when they talk to their unborn child.

Rachel's boss at Central Perk is named Terry.

By their sixth date, Paolo had given names to both of Rachel's breasts.

Monica once threw a plate after losing at Pictionary.

Ursula stole Phoebe's boyfriend, Randy Brown.

The Bobcats were the mascot of Rachel, Monica, and Ross's high school.

Chandler's secretary had breast-reduction surgery on just one breast.

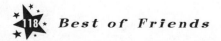

30. The One with the Time Line

★★

TIMES OF THEIR LIVES

September 22, 1994: *Friends* premieres from 8:30 to 9:00 P.M. (EST) between *Mad About You* and *Seinfeld* on NBC.

January 27, 1995: Cast members grace cover of *Entertainment Weekly*

February 11, 1995: Jennifer Aniston's twenty-sixth birthday

April 17, 1995: *Friends* on cover of *People*

March 2, 1995: *Friends* is given the prime-time slot from 9:30 to 10:00 P.M. (EST), sandwiched between *Seinfeld* and the top-rated *ER*.

May 8, 1995: Courteney Cox on cover of *People*'s "50 Most Beautiful People in the World 1995" issue

May 18, 1995: Cast members featured on cover of *Rolling Stone*

May 25, 1995: The Rembrandts give first live performance of *Friends* theme, "I'll Be There for You" on *Late Night with Conan O'Brien*.

May 27, 1995: Lisa Kudrow becomes the first Friend to get married when she weds French ad-exec Michel Stern in Malibu. All of her fellow cast members, except for David Schwimmer, who was filming *The Pallbearer* in New York, attended.

June 6, 1995: Jennifer Aniston guests on *The Tonight Show*. She brings out Kareem Abdul-Jabbar to help her do basketball tricks.

June 15, 1995: Courteney Cox and Jon Lovitz host *1995 MTV Movie Awards*. The duo open the show by parodying Des'ree's hit song "You Gotta Be." Courteney plays drums and sings off-key. This is also Courteney's thirty-first birthday.

June 19–25, 1995 (week of): A rerun of *Friends* is the number one overall show in America, topping *ER* and *Seinfeld*. *Friends* remains the top show for most of summer.

June 22, 1995: Jennifer Aniston and Lisa Kudrow co-host *VH-1 Honors* after Greg Kinnear drops out.

July 17, 1995: Matthew Perry guest-stars on the *Late Show with David Lettterman*. He's the first cast member to be on a chat show *after Friends* hits number one in the Nielsen ratings.

July 19, 1995: The Rembrandts win Beatle-esque screams after performing "I'll Be There for You" on *The Tonight Show*. Quite impressive, especially considering that the main attraction that night was hunky Boy Wonder, Chris O'Donnell.

July 20, 1995: *Friends* is nominated for eight Emmys, including best comedy series. Although all six of the actors submitted entries to be considered for best supporting actor and best supporting actress, only David Schwimmer and Lisa Kudrow won nominations.

July 25, 1995: Matt LeBlanc's twenty-eighth birthday

July 26, 1995: David Schwimmer takes a break from filming *The Pallbearer* to appear with David Letterman on *Late Show*.

July 27, 1995: Back in California, Matt LeBlanc is doing the chat show circuit with Jay Leno on *The Tonight Show*.

July 30, 1995: Lisa Kudrow's thirty-second birthday

Aug. 19, 1995: Matthew Perry's twenty-sixth birthday

Aug. 24, 1995: Confident that *Friends* is strong enough to survive a weaker time period, NBC moves the show to its new time slot: 8:00 to 8:30 P.M. (EST).

Sept. 10, 1995: *Friends* sets out to win trophies at its first Emmy Awards

Sept. 21, 1995: The second season of *Friends* begins

Nov. 12, 1995: David Schwimmer's twenty-ninth birthday

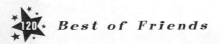

The One About the Author

Jae-Ha Kim is the pop-culture reporter for the *Chicago Sun-Times* and has one *New York Times* bestseller under her belt. Kim received her B.A. from the University of Chicago and her M.S. from Northwestern University, which *Friends* star David Schwimmer also attended. In a perfect world, she would meet a man who has Chandler's wit, Joey's looks, and Ross's kind heart. But she would settle for Brad Pitt.

(Daniel DuVerney)